Bilingual

Japanese / English

知的財産権の ガイドブック

Intellectual Property Rights

Guidebook

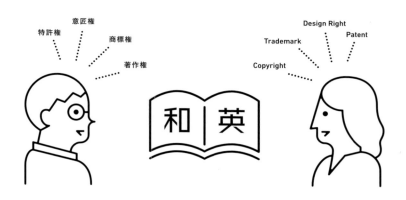

特許権　意匠権　商標権　著作権　和｜英　Design Right　Patent　Trademark　Copyright

渡邉知子

弁理士

WATANABE Tomoko

Patent Attorney

一般社団法人　発明推進協会

JIPII

はじめに

従前、知的財産権に関する業務は、弁理士または弁護士などの専門家、企業内では特許部または法務部により扱われ、営業などの一般のビジネスパーソンにはあまり馴染みのない知識でした。しかしインターネット、SNSなどデジタル技術の普及により、情報の伝達、普及速度が急速に早まり、現在知的財産権は、一般のビジネスパーソンにとっても必要、かつ重要な基礎知識となっています。学部を問わず大学などの全ての学生にも将来の自身のビジネスおよびキャリア形成に必要な学習すべき内容となっています。

例えば、ネット上の他者の著作物を簡単にコピーして使用できる現状下では、他者の著作物をコピーして使用できる範囲の制限など、著作権に関する基礎知識は企業に限らず個人にも必須な知識です。

他の知的財産権は、特にビジネスにおいては必須です。例えば、
・企業では、商品またはサービスの企画会議において、まだ内容が明確になる前の自社商品のポジショニングを考える段階から、権利侵害を避けるため、競合他社が保有する特許権や意匠権をインターネットで簡易に調査し検討することが行われています。
・新規ネーミングやキャッチフレーズを検討する際には商標の簡易調査をしながら検討することが行われています。
・営業の現場では、自社商品をアピールするための自社が保有する技術に関する特許の理解、デザインに関する意匠権の理解なども不可欠です。

加えて、グローバルな市場におけるビジネスには、英語による知的財産権の知識も必須です。

Introduction

In the past, the work related to Intellectual Property (IP) rights was handled by experts such as patent attorneys or lawyers. Within a company, the patent department or the legal department handled these matters, while non-legal related staff did not. However, the situation has recently changed due to the new digital technologies, such as the Internet and SNS platforms, that facilitate a faster transmission of information. These days, knowledge of IP rights is essential for businesspeople. All university students, regardless of major or grade, need a basic knowledge of IP rights for their future career or business.

For example, copyright applies not only to businesspeople but actually everyone. It is essential, especially under the present circumstances where data can be copied easily, to possess fundamental knowledge of copyright, in order to avoid issues with existing copyrighted works.

The other IP rights mainly apply to the business world. For instance:
· For companies planning new products or services, it is a common practice to perform general online research on their competitors IP rights during the planning stage.
· IP rights research is necessary when naming products, creating catch phrases or coming up with trademarks in order to avoid IP rights violations.
· Regarding sales activities, it is essential for sales staff to have a sufficient understanding of the patents related to technology and design rights owned by their company in order to promote their products to their customers.

In addition, knowledge of IP rights in English is also essential for doing business in the global market.

このような背景を踏まえ、一般のビジネスパーソンにとって必要な知的財産権に関する基礎知識および情報、または専門家に相談する前段階の知識として役立つような知的財産権のガイドラインとして本書を日本語と英語の両方の言語でまとめることにしました。忙しい状況の中でも短時間で理解でき、かつ必要な時にすぐに確認できるよう、コンパクトで分かり易い内容および構成を目指しました。本書は日本法を中核とするものですが、必要と思われる外国法（米国、EU、中国）、また国際制度や条約についても触れています。

本書が皆様にとって知的財産権に対する理解の一助になれば幸いです。

渡邉 知子

The following background, basic knowledge, and information on IP rights is vital for general businesspeople work and consult efficiently with IP specialists. I wrote this book in two languages to provide both Japanese and English-speaking audiences clear guidance on IP rights during the early consulting steps. I aimed at writing a compact and easy-to-understand guide, paying attention to its contents and structure. This book is mainly based on Japanese law, but also touches on other countries' laws (USA, EU, and China), international systems, and treaties.

I sincerely hope this book will help everyone to gain a better understanding of Intellectual Property rights.

WATANABE Tomoko

本書の基本形式

本書は、左右見開きのページに、同じ内容で左ページに日本語、右ページに英語を掲載しました。これにより、日本語と英語の置き換えが容易にできるため、どちらかの言語で内容を理解できれば、他方の言語に置き換えることができ、知的財産権の基本的な知識を日本語と英語で学習することができます。また、日本語または英語を理解する人々の間における知的財産権に関するコミュニケーショに役立てることができます。本書の後半には復習のための事例問題を付しました。基本的な事例問題を用いて具体的に考えてみることにより、知的財産権のわかりにくい側面を補い、理解を深めることを意図しています。加えて、日本語と英語の基本用語の一覧表、および参考情報のURLを付けました。

この本の翻訳ついて：
本書は、日本語・英語のどちらの言語においても理解しやすいことを最優先にしています。例えば説明の仕方や順序などは異なる場合がありますが、内容や意味は同じです。

Basic format of this book

In this book, Japanese is on the left page and English is on the right page. This format allows quick and easy access for both Japanese and English audiences. In addition, this book should prove very useful when speakers of different languages discuss about IP rights-related topics. There are some case-study questions to support your review on IP rights after the last chapter of this book. This will help to consolidate your understanding of the contents and to clarify complicated points. In addition, there is a table of "Basic Terms" in English and Japanese, followed by URL references.

A note regarding the translation of this book:
Some words or phrases may differ in the Japanese and in the English pages, yet the contents will be the same.

目　次

第1章　知的財産権の概要

第2章　5種類の権利

第3章　出願から登録

Contents

Chapter 1　IP Rights Outline

Chapter 2　The Five Rights

Chapter 3　Application to Registration

第4章　保護期間

第5章　国際出願

第6章　その他

復習・資料

Chapter 4　Protection Period

Chapter 5　International Application

Chapter 6　Other Issues

Review & Resources

知 的 財 産 権 の 概 要

IP Rights Outline

知的財産とは？

知的財産は、創作性のある文学、芸術作品、発明、デザイン、そしてシンボル、商業上用いられる名前やイメージです。知的財産は、例えば、著作権、特許権、実用新案権、意匠権、商標権、地理的表示などのように、一定の条件下で法律により権利として保護されます。知的財産により、クリエイターは自身の作品が認知されたり、金銭的な利益を得ることができます。　クリエイターの利益とより広い公衆の利益との間の良いバランスを見つけることにより、創造性とイノベーションが繁栄できる環境を作り出します。また、模倣の防止を図り、商取引の信用維持に貢献します。

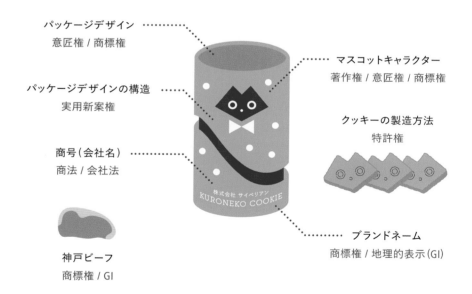

パッケージデザイン
意匠権 / 商標権

マスコットキャラクター
著作権 / 意匠権 / 商標権

パッケージデザインの構造
実用新案権

クッキーの製造方法
特許権

商号（会社名）
商法 / 会社法

ブランドネーム
商標権 / 地理的表示(GI)

神戸ビーフ
商標権 / GI

・実用新案権は、制度がある国とない国があります。
・知的財産を保護する法律は、上記の他に、不正競争防止法、半導体集積回路の回路配置に関する法律、種苗法などもあります。

What is Intellectual Property?

Intellectual Property (IP) refers to creations of the mind, such as: literary and artistic works, inventions, designs and symbols, names and images used in commerce. IP is protected under the law (such as copyright, patents, utility model rights, design rights, trademarks and geographical indications) and enables creators to be given recognition or gain financial benefit from their creations. Finding a good balance between the interests of creators and the wider public allows an environment where creativity and innovation can flourish. It also prevents counterfeiting and contributes to maintaining credibility in commerce.

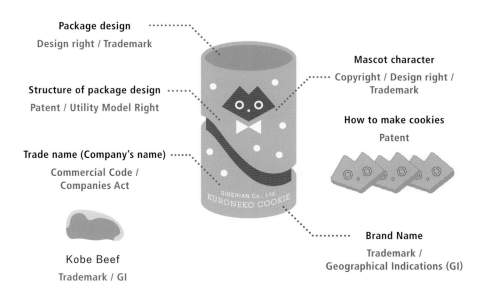

Package design
Design right / Trademark

Structure of package design
Patent / Utility Model Right

Trade name (Company's name)
Commercial Code / Companies Act

Kobe Beef
Trademark / GI

Mascot character
Copyright / Design right / Trademark

How to make cookies
Patent

SIBERIAN Co., Ltd.
KURONEKO COOKIE

Brand Name
Trademark / Geographical Indications (GI)

· Some countries have a "utility model rights" system, other countries do not.
· Some other acts related to IP protection are "Unfair Competition Prevention Act", "Act on the Circuit Layout of Semiconductor Integrated Circuits", and "Plant Variety Protection and Seed Act", etc.

知的財産権の概要 (1)

知的財産権は、法律で権利としての保護を図ることにより、権利の創作者や権利者に対し利益をもたらし、新たな芸術や産業への投資を促進させます。新たな創作やイノベーションの創出を奨励し、商取引の信用維持を図り、文化および経済の発展による豊かな社会の実現に貢献するものです。日本の知的財産権は、以下のように保護する権利ごとに法律が分かれています。

著作権　-　著作権法
特許権　-　特許法
実用新案権　-　実用新案法
意匠権　-　意匠法
商標権　-　商標法
地理的表示(GI)　-　地理的表示(GI)法 *

不正競争防止法

産業財産権(特許権、実用新案権、意匠権、商標権)を取得するためには、特許庁(官庁)への出願、および登録手続きが必要です。これらの手続きには費用が必要です。登録された権利を維持するためにも年金の支払いが必要です。

一方、著作権は、官庁への出願、および登録手続きは必要ありません。
これらのルールは世界共通です。

上記の他に、「半導体集積回路の回路配置に関する法律」、「種苗法」などの法律により保護されている知的財産権もあります。

* 地理的表示法の正式名称は、「特定農林水産物等の名称の保護に関する法律」です。

IP Rights Outline (1)

Intellectual Property (IP) rights deliver benefits to creators and owners through legal protection, promoting and encouraging investments in new artistic creations and industrial innovations. As a result, IP rights benefit society by enriching the culture and growing the economy. Japanese IP rights are divided into individual laws:

Copyright	-	Copyright Act
Patents	-	Patent Act
Utility Model rights	-	Utility Model Act
Design rights	-	Design Act
Trademarks	-	Trademark Act
Geographical Indications (GI)	-	Geographical Indication (GI) Act*

Unfair Competition Prevention Act

Industrial property rights (patents, utility model rights, design rights, and trademarks) must be applied for and registered with the Patent Office (government office). The applicant must pay application fees in order to apply and register for the rights. Maintaining the right requires additional annual fees.

However, these processes and fees do not apply to copyright.
All of these rules apply globally.

Some other Acts of IP rights are "Act on the Circuit Layout of Semiconductor Integrated Circuits", "Plant Variety Protection and Seed Act" and so on.

* GI Act's official name: Protection of the Names of Specific Agricultural, Forestry and Fishery Products and Foodstuffs Act.

知的財産権の概要 (2)

知的財産権(法)は、権利および法律の性質により以下のカテゴリーに大別されます。

著作権 / 産業財産権
・思想または感情を創作的に表現した文芸、音楽、美術などの著作物を保護する著作権
・産業財産権である、特許権、実用新案権、意匠権、商標権

創作促進法 / 営業標識法
・知的創作物を保護する著作権法、特許法、実用新案法、意匠法
・市場におけるビジネスの安定を図るための商標法、地理的表示法、不正競争防止法

相対的独占権 / 絶対的独占権
・著作権は、相対的独占権といわれ、他人が独自に創作したものには権利は及びません。独自に創作された著作物は保護されるため、偶然同一、または近似する作品が作成されても著作権侵害とはなりません。著作権侵害は、他者の著作物に依拠し、かつ類似した創作がなされた時に成立します。不正競争防止法上の利益も著作権同様、他人が独自に創作したものには及びません。
・産業財産権は、絶対的独占権といわれ、著作権とは異なり、権利の存在を知っていたか否かに関わらず、侵害が成立します。したがって権利侵害を避けるには、事前に他者の所有する権利調査が必要です。また、産業財産権は先願主義に基づいた権利なので、先に特許庁へ出願した者に権利が与えられます。

IP Rights Outline (2)

IP rights and acts are divided into distinct categories:

Copyright / Industrial Property Rights
· Copyright protects any production in which thoughts or sentiments are expressed in a creative way, such as creations from literary, scientific, artistic or musical domain.
· Industrial property rights are patents, utility model rights, design rights and trademarks.

Encouraging creations of the mind / Maintaining business trust
· Protection of creations: Copyright Act, Patent Act, Utility Model Act, and Design Act.
· Maintaining stable business in the marketplace: Trademark Act, GI Act, Unfair Competition Prevention Act

Relative monopoly / Absolute monopoly
· Copyright is a relative monopoly. Copyright does not cover the other author's original work. Copyrighted works created independently are protected. Identical works created independently and coincidentally similar are not an infringement. When a creation is based on the work of others and similarity exists, then infringement occurs. Benefits gained by the Unfair Competition Prevention Act as well as by copyright do not cover the work of others.
· Industrial property rights which are an exclusive monopoly. Infringement occurs regardless of whether a party knew of the existence of prior rights or not. Therefore, in order to avoid infringement, it is necessary to search the rights of others in advance. Industrial property rights are based on the first-file rule. Therefore, the applicant who files earlier becomes the owner of the right.

知的財産権の概要 (3)

知的財産権					
	産業財産権				
目的	知的創作物を保護する法律				市場におけるビジネスの安定を図るための法律
法律	著作権法	特許法	実用新案法	意匠法	商標法	不正競争防止法
権利	著作権	特許権	実用新案権	意匠権	商標権	不正競争行為の防止
主な保護対象	文芸、音楽、美術、映画、写真、コンピュータプログラム	物の構造、生産方法、ビジネスモデル、コンピュータソフトウエア	物の構造	量産品、建築物、内装、画像のデザイン	ロゴ、マーク（図形）、音、ホログラム、色	営業秘密など、不正競争行為と規定されたもの*
出願・登録	不要	必要				不要
権利の特徴	相対的独占権	絶対的独占権				相対的独占権
権利の効果	権利の譲渡・ライセンス					―
	侵害行為に対する差し止め・損害賠償請求					

保護対象は国により異なるので、各国における保護対象の確認が必要です。

*86ページ参照

IP Rights Outline (3)

Intellectual Property Rights					
			Industrial Property Rights		
Purpouse	Protection for the intellectual creation				Stable business in the market
Act	Copyright Act	Patent Act	Utility Model Act	Design Act	Trademark Act	Unfair Competition Prevention Act
Right	Copyright	Patents	Utility Model rights	Design rights	Trademarks	Prevention for Unfair Competition acts
Main objects	Novels, Music, Paintings, Movies, Photos, Computer programs	Product mechanism, Methods of production, Business models, Computer software	Product mechanism	Mass production products, Buildings, Interior designs, Graphic images on screen	Logos, Marks (Figures), Sounds, Holograms, Colors	Trade secrets etc., that are defined as unfair competition*
Filing Registration	Not necessary	Necessary				Not necessary
Feature of the right	Relative monopoly	Absolute monopoly				Relative monopoly
Effect	Rights of transfer / Licences					—
	Requirement to obtain injunction and demand compensation for damages					

Protected objects vary from country to country. Therefore, it is essential to confirm which objects are protected in a particular country.
* See 87 page

5種類の権利

The Five Rights

著作権 (1)

著作権とは?

著作権(または著作者の権利)は、クリエイターの文芸および芸術的な作品(著作物)の権利に対して使用される法律用語です。

著作権により保護されるものは何か?

通常法律には、著作物を余すことなく記載したリストの記載はありません。しかし一般的に世界中において著作権で保護されるものには以下のものが含まれます。

小説・詩のような文芸作品、演劇、新聞記事

コンピュータープログラム、データベース

映画、作曲、振り付け

絵画、建築物、広告、地図
製図、写真、彫刻

著作権は表現にのみ保護が及び、アイデア、手順、創作方法、数学的概念のようなものは保護されません。

著作権には著作物として十分な要件を揃えているか否かにより、保護対象となり得るか否かが決まるものがあります。例えばタイトル、スローガン、ロゴなどです。

Copyright (1)

What is copyright?

Copyright (or author's right) is a legal term used to describe the rights that creators have over their literary and artistic works.

What can be protected using Copyright?

Exhaustive lists of works covered by copyright are usually not found in legislation. Nonetheless, broadly speaking, works commonly protected by copyright worldwide include:

Literary works such as novels, poems, plays, newspaper articles

Computer programs, databases

Films, musical compositions, choreography

Artistic works such as paintings, drawings, architecture, advertisements, maps
Technical drawings, photographs, sculpture

Copyright protection extends only to expressions and not to ideas, procedures, methods of operation or mathematical concepts.

Copyright may or may not be applicable to a number of objects such as titles, slogans or logos, depending on whether they contain sufficient authorship or not.

著作権 (2)

著作権の特徴

著作者の権利には2種の権利が含まれます。
・財産権としての著作権
・人格権としての著作者人格権

財産権としての著作権には以下の多岐にわたる様々な権利が含まれます。
複製権、上演および演奏権、上映権、公衆送信権、口述権、展示権、頒布権、譲渡権、
貸与権、翻訳権、翻案権、その他実演家のための著作隣接権、出版権など

著作権の制限

以下の著作物の使用は著作権侵害とはなりません。
私的利用、図書館における複製、引用、教科書用図書への掲載、学校教育番組の放送、
教育機関における複製、試験問題としての複製、視覚障害者のための複製、聴覚障害者
のための複製、営利を目的としない上映、時事問題に関する論説の転載、政治上の演説
の利用、時事の事件の報道のための利用、美術の著作物等の展示に伴う複製、情報解
析のための複製など

著作権は登録できる?

大半の国では、ベルヌ条約＊によって著作権による保護は登録または他の形式的要件無
しに、自動的に与えられます。それに関わらず、ほとんどの国では作品の任意登録を可
能にするためのシステムが整っています。そのような任意登録システムは、権利者また
は創作をめぐる紛争を解決するのに役立つだけでなく、金融取引、販売、ならびに権利
に関する契約および／または譲渡を容易にしています。WIPO（68ページ参照）は著作
権登録システムや検索可能な著作権データベースは提供していません。

＊ベルヌ条約については、68ページ参照

Copyright (2)

Features of Copyright

The author's rights include two kinds of rights.
· Economic rights = Property right
· Moral rights = Personal nature

Economic rights include various rights:
The right of reproduction, stage performance rights and musical performance rights, the right of screen presentation, the right of public transmission (broadcast to the public), recitation rights, exhibition rights, distribution rights, the right of ownership transfer, the right of rental, translation and adaptation rights, the right of the original author in the exploitation of a derivative work, neighboring rights, the right of publication, etc.

Limitations on Copyright

The following activities are not a copyright infringement:
Reproduction for private use, reproduction in libraries, quotations, reproduction of school textbook, reproduction in order to prepare a textbook in large print, broadcasts in school education programs, reproduction made by schools and other educational institutions, reproduction in examination questions, reproduction for the visually and hearing impaired, nonprofit performances, reproduction of editorials on current topics, use in political speech, reporting of current events, exhibition of an artistic work by the owner of the original, exploitation of an artistic work located in open space, duplication for information analysis, etc.

Can Copyright be Registered?

In the majority of countries, in accordance with the Berne Convention*, copyright protection is obtained automatically without the need for registration or other formalities.
However, most countries also have a system in place for the voluntary copyright registration. These systems can help solve disputes over ownership or creation, as well as facilitating financial transactions, sales and assignment and / or transfer of rights. WIPO (see page 69) does not offer a copyright registration system or a searchable copyright database.

* regarding Berne Convention: see page 69

特許権

日本の特許法は、発明を自然法則を利用した技術的創作のうち高度なものと定義し、産業の発達に寄与することを目的としています。

保護対象
特許法では、新たな方法によって作られる製品またはそのプロセス、課題に対する新たな技術的解決法を保護します。例えば、製品の仕組み、構造、製造方法、ビジネスモデル、コンピュータソフトウェアです。

出願公開と審査請求
特許は出願公開制度を採用しており、通常、出願から1年半後に全ての出願が公開されます。審査請求により審査に着手され、出願から3年以内に審査請求を行わなければ、出願は取下げとなります。

登録要件
審査請求された出願は、審査官が登録要件を満たすか否かの審査を行います。登録要件には、主に新規性と進歩性があります。発明が世界公知、公用の場合、新規性が無いと判断され、拒絶になります*。新規性の判断基準は出願日です。進歩性は、特許出願前にその発明の属する技術の分野における通常の知識を有する者が公知の発明に基いて容易に発明をすることができたと判断された場合に進歩性が無いとして、拒絶になります。特許発明の技術的範囲（権利範囲）は、特許請求の範囲の記載に基づいて定められます。

---

*新規性喪失の例外規定として、自己の公開から1年以内の出願について救済規定があります。

Patents

According to the Japanese Patent Act, an invention is a highly advanced technical creation which utilizes natural laws and contributes to the development of industry.

Protected Objects

Products / processes that provide a new way of doing something or that offer a new technical solution to a problem - such as a product mechanism, a structure, a production method, a business model, or computer software - are inventions protected by the Patent Act.

Publication of the Application and Examination Request

Patents use an open system in which almost all applications are published one and a half years after the application date. An application is withdrawn unless a request for examination is submitted within 3 years of the application date.

Registration Requirements

Examination requests must meet the registration requirements (mainly novelty and inventive steps). If the invention is publicly known around the world before the application date, it is judged that there is no novelty and the application will be rejected*. It is judged that there is no inventive step when an average person in a particular field can easily create the invention with publicly available technical knowledge prior to the application date. The technical scope of protection for a patent consists of the claims in the application document.

---

* Exceptions exist when novelty has been lost due to self-publication of the invention before application date.
  However, filing must take place within one year of the publication date.

実用新案権

日本の実用新案法は、物品の形状、構造または組合せに係る考案を保護し、産業の発達に寄与することを目的としています。

保護対象

実用新案法の保護対象は物品の形状、構造または組合せに限られ、これらは特許法と重複しています。ただし、コンピュータプログラム、製造方法、ビジネスモデルなどは、特許法によってのみ保護されます。

無審査

実用新案法の特許法との大きな相違は、新規性などの実体審査が行われず、無審査登録制度を採用している点です。実用新案制度では実体審査は行われませんが、出願と登録の手続きは必要です。これにより、早期に権利が発生します。

技術評価書

権利行使する際は、相手方に対し特許庁審査官が作成する「技術評価書」の提示が必要です。これは、登録された実用新案権の有効性についての客観的な判断材料となるもので、特許庁の審査官が先行技術文献の調査を行って新規性、進歩性などについて評価するものです。「技術評価書」は出願後いつでも請求することができます。また、権利者ではない第三者も請求することができます。

Utility Model Rights

In Japan, the Utility Model Act protects creation of technical ideas related to the shape and structure of the products or a combination of both and contributes to the development of industry.

Protected Objects

The above objects can be protected by both the Utility Model Act and the Patent Act. However, computer programs, methods of production, business models and so on, are only protected by the Patent Act and not by the Utility Model Act.

No Examination

The Utility Model Act differs from the Patent Act because substantive examination, such as novelty, is not conducted. The utility model rights system is not subject to examination, but application and registration are required. Utility model rights are registered much more promptly, because substantive examinations are not carried out.

Technical Evaluation Document

When exercising the right, it is necessary to present a "Technical Evaluation Document" prepared by an examiner. This is an objective source of judgment on the validity of the registered utility model right. The examiner examines the prior art documents and evaluates the novelty and inventive step. "Technical Evaluation Document" can be requested by right holders, other parties, and also any other member of the public. It can be requested at any time after application.

意匠権 (1)

日本の意匠法は、意匠(デザイン)の保護および利用を図ることにより創作を奨励し、産業の発達に寄与することを目的としています。

保護対象

意匠法の保護対象は、量産可能な物品などの意匠(デザイン)です。工業製品全般を保護し、各種機器、家具、パッケージ、部品、付属品、および菓子などの食品も含まれます。また、建築物、内装デザイン、画像デザインも保護されます。

登録要件

権利を取得するためには、特許庁へ出願し、出願後、全件について審査官が登録要件を満たすか否かの審査を行います。登録要件には、主に新規性[*1]と創作性があります。出願意匠(デザイン)が世界公知、公用の意匠と同一または類似する場合、新規性が無いと判断され、拒絶になります。新規性の判断基準は出願日です。創作性は、当業者が日本国内または外国において、公知の意匠に基づいて容易に意匠の創作をすることができたと判断された場合、創作容易と判断され、拒絶の対象になります。
意匠の権利範囲は、登録意匠およびこれに類似する意匠に及びます。

部分意匠 [*2]

物品の形態全体のデザインに加え、物品の一部を請求し、登録することができます。例えば、自動車のフロント部分のみを部分意匠として登録することができます(36ページ参照)。

ヨーロッパ諸国など、新規性、創作性等の実体審査を行っていない国々もあります。
[*1] 新規性喪失の例外規定として、自己の公開から1年以内の出願について救済規定があります。
[*2] 部分意匠制度を採用していない国もあります。

Design Rights (1)

The Japanese Design Act aims to protect creativity in order to encourage innovative design so as to contribute to the development of industry.

Protected objects

The Design Act protects design of mass-produced products and so on. It protects industrial products in general, including equipment, furniture, product packages, components, parts, and foods such as confectionery. Also, buildings, interior designs and graphic images of screen design are protected by this Act.

Registration Requirements

In order to acquire the right, you must make an application. After filing, all applications are examined by an examiner. The right is registered if the application satisfies all necessary requirements. Registration requirements are primarily novelty[1] and creativity. If the design is publicly known around the world before the application date, it is judged that there is no novelty and the application will be rejected. It is judged that there is no creativity if a person in a particular field can easily create the design with publicly available knowledge prior to the application date. The scope of protection of design rights is the registered design and also its similar designs.

Partial Design[2]

In addition to protecting the whole product design, you can also register a partial design. For example, it is possible to register only the front part of a car as a partial design (see page 36).

There are countries, such as European countries, that do not examine novelty, creativity, etc.
[1] Exceptions exist when novelty has been lost due to self-publication of the design before filing. However, filing must take place within one year of your publication date.
[2] Some countries do not have a partial-design system.

意匠権 (2)

日本の意匠法には、デザインの保護を有効に行うため、以下のような制度もあります。

関連意匠制度

意匠の創作過程では、複数のデザインバリエーションを創作しながら、最終的に商品化するデザインを決定します。また、商品化が決定されたデザイン案も製品化の過程で製造上の理由などにより、デザインが多少変更されることがあります。商品の発売後は、自動車業界に代表されるようにデザインコンセプトを保持しながらモデルチェンジが行なわれます。このようなデザイン創作特有の事情を踏まえ、より幅広くデザインを保護しするために、関連意匠制度があります。この制度を利用できるのは、同一の出願人または権利者による類似する意匠出願で、かつ最初の本意匠の出願日から10年以内の出願です。

秘密意匠制度 *

出願意匠が登録されると、公報が発行されます。日本の意匠制度は、登録前に出願が公開されない（ハーグ／国際デザインシステムによる出願 * を除く。72,76ページ参照）ため、他者は登録公報により登録意匠を知ることになります。しかし、デザインは模倣されやすいため、出願人が秘密意匠を請求することにより、公報の発行時に、意匠に係る物品、説明および意匠を非公開とすることができます。非公開の期間は、登録から最長3年間です。秘密期間終了後、通常の公報が発行されます。秘密意匠の請求は、出願時、または登録料の納付と同時に行うことができます。秘密意匠の権利行使は、相手方に登録意匠を提示し警告した上でなければすることができません。

* ハーグ／国際デザインシステムによる出願は、この制度は利用できません。

Design Rights (2)

The Japanese Design Act has other systems. These systems are useful protection of the design.

Related Design System

During the design creation process, more than one design is made, but only one will become the final product. However, due to production issues, the chosen design might change some of its details. For example, in the car industry, after the product launch, the design concept might be kept but its color and other minor details might change in later versions. Considering these circumstances, the "Related Design System" was created in order to more broadly protect the design concept. When using this system, it is important to submit applications that meet certain conditions. Same holder or applicant and similar designs to the original design. You can register more designs as related designs, as long as making the application within ten years of the application date of the first-filed original design.

Secret Design System*

After the registration, the design will be published by an official gazette. Under the Japanese design system, there is no publication for applied design (excluding HAGUE / International design system application. See 72,76 pages), third party can check registered designs in an official gazette. Applicants can apply to keep secret due to risk of imitation. If applicant apply for secret design, the article of the product, design explanation and drawings will not made public. The period of secrecy is a maximum of 3 years from the registration date. After the end of the period, a usual official gazette will be published. There are two chances to apply for secret design, one is at the same time as filing and the other is at the same time as the registration fee payment. If you use the right of secret design, you must send a warning letter with your application to the opposite party.

* HAGUE / International design system application can not use this system.

意匠権 (3) / Design Rights (3)

日本国特許庁により様々なデザインが登録されています
Various designs are registered by the Japan Patent Office (JPO)

No. は日本の意匠登録番号です
"No." is the Japanese design registration number

トヨタ自動車株式会社
TOYOTA MOTOR CORPORATION
乗用自動車
Car

No.1613298

全体意匠 / Whole design

No.1613299

部分意匠 / Partial design

株式会社 イトーキ
Itoki, Inc
テーブル
Table

No.1625894

本意匠 / Original design

No.1626094

関連意匠 / Related design

アップル インコーポレイテッド
Apple Inc.
携帯情報端末
Mobile phone

No.1498958

部分意匠 / Partial design

No.1498959

部分意匠 / Partial design

No.1514007

ダイソン テクノロジー リミテッド
Dyson Technology Limited
ヘアードライヤー
Hair dryer

No.1603816

株式会社良品計画
Ryohin Keikaku Co., Ltd.
アロマストーン
Aroma stone

No.1397477

アッシュコンセプト株式会社
H Concept Co., Ltd.
輪ゴム
Rubber band

No.1478077

株式会社ワコール
Wacoal corp.
スポーツ用タイツ
Sports tights

No.1549638

本田技研工業株式会社
HONDA MOTOR CO.,LTD
自動車用ステアリングホイール
Car steering wheel

No.1610882

ソニー株式会社
SONY CORPORATION
ロボット
Robot

No.1216510
部分意匠 / Partial design

サントリー株式会社
SUNTORY LIMITED
包装用容器
Package

No.1181642

株式会社グランビル
Groundbuil Corporation
組み立て家屋
Mass-produced house

No.1593941

ゴディバ
GODIVA BELGIUM B.V.B./S.P.R.L.
チョコレート
Chocolates

商標権 (1)

商標法は名称やマーク、図形（またはこれらの結合）などを商品や役務（サービス）ごとに登録し、使用者の業務上の信用維持を図ることにより、産業の発達に寄与し、あわせて需要者の利益を保護するための法律です。特許法や意匠法などの創作保護法とは異なる性質を持ち、商標の創作そのものに価値を与えず、商標を継続使用することにより得られる、業務上の信用に重きを置きます。

商標の機能
商標は、出所識別機能、品質表示機能、広告機能の三大機能を有し、ブランド価値および企業価値の形成に不可欠です。

指定商品・役務
商品・役務に関する国際分類（ニース分類）により、商品または役務が 45 の区分（クラス）に分かれています。出願する際に、指定商品または役務、およびそれらが属する区分を指定する必要があります。

登録要件
商標の登録には、その標章を自己の業務で提供している商品や役務に使用して自他商品・役務の識別力を有することが必要です。例えば、商品の産地や品質などを普通に使用した商標は登録できません。また、すでに登録または出願されている他人の商標または類似する商標をその商標と同じ、または類似する指定商品または役務に使用する商標も拒絶の対象となります。つまり、商品・役務が非類似であれば同一の商標でも登録されます（43 ページ参照）。権利範囲は、指定商品または指定役務についての登録商標の使用に及びますが、同一または類似する指定商品または指定役務についての同一または類似する登録商標の使用も侵害とみなされます（禁止権の範囲）。商標権の権利期間は、10 年毎の更新により半永久的に権利を保有することができます。

普通名称化した商標
登録商標であっても他者がその商標を多用することにより識別力が失われ、普通名称化した場合、権利の効力が失われます。例えば、エスカレータ、ポケットベルなどが該当します。

Trademarks (1)

The Trademark Act protects a distinctive logo, name, mark, figure (or a combination of these items) of certain goods or services produced or provided by an individual or a company. The system helps consumers identify and purchase a product or service based on whether its specific characteristics, trust and quality, and contribution to the development of industry – as indicated by its unique trademark– meet their needs.

Trademark Functions

Trademarks have three major functions: identification, quality indication and advertisement. All are indispensable when forming brand and corporate value.

Designated Goods / Services

The international classification for goods and services (NICE classification) has 45 classes. When filing an application, it is necessary to clearly state which classes of goods or services the trademark covers.

Registration Requirements

Registration of trademarks requires the mark to possess distinctiveness among other trademarks in the same field of business. For example, you cannot register trademarks that use words that commonly refer to the product's origin or quality etc. If a trademark is the same or is judged to be similar to another trademark which has the same or similar designated goods or services, then the application will be rejected. On the other hand, if the designated goods or services are not similar then the application will be accepted, even though the trademarks are the same (see page 43). Similarity is judged by reviewing the overall effect of all three criteria combined. Trademarks have two types of scope. The scope of protection is when both the trademark and the designated goods or services are the same; when another trademark, designated goods or services are similar to the protected item, it will be prohibited. Both scopes are fully protected by Trademark Act. Trademark protection can be renewed every 10 years in perpetuity.

Common Trademarks

Trademarks can become invalid over time if a trademark becomes a common word used by many people and has lost its distinctiveness. For example, "escalator", "pager" etc.

商標権 (2)

文字や図形、記号からなる商標に加え、現在では以下にあげるように様々なタイプの商標が、日本の商標法により保護されています。

立体商標

立体形状も商標として登録することができます。ただし、商品または商品の包装が当然に備えている特徴のみから成る商標は登録することはできません。

音商標

音商標は、音楽、音声、自然音など、聴覚で認識される音の商標です。例えば、CMで使用されるサウンドロゴなどです。

動き商標

動き商標は、文字や図形などが時間の経過に伴って変化する商標で、例えば、変化するロゴなどです。

ホログラム商標

ホログラム商標は、文字や図形などがホログラフィーやその他の方法により、見る角度によって変化する商標です。

色彩のみからなる商標

色彩のみからなる商標は、単色または複数の色彩の組合せのみからなる商標です。

位置商標

位置商標は、文字や図形などを商品などにつける位置が特定される商標です。

地域団体商標

事業共同組合などが登録することのできる、需要者の間に広く認識されている商標で、その構成員のみがその商標を使用することができます。例えば、今治タオルなど。

防護商標

既に需要者の間で広く認識されている商標を、登録されている指定商品・役務とは非類似の商品・役務について、他人が使用することにより混同を生じる恐れがあるとき、権利者は防護商標としてこれらを登録することができます。つまり防護商標の登録により、未然に非類似の商品・役務について他者が登録することを防ぐことができます。

Trademarks (2)

Logos, figures, and marks have been protected and nowadays various types of trademarks, such as those below, can be protected under the Japanese Trademark Act.

Three Dimensional Trademarks

Three dimensional shapes are protected by this Act. However, if the products or packages consist of only indistinct general forms, shapes or features, then these cannot be registered.

Sound Trademarks

Music, vocal sounds, natural sounds, and all other sounds, which can be heard, are protected by this Act. For example, a sound logo which is used by an advertisement or commercial.

Motion Trademarks

Motion trademarks are logos, figures, etc. that change their shape, color or size during a given period of time, for example, an animated logo.

Hologram Trademarks

Hologram trademarks are logos or figures, etc. that use holographic or other methods to alter their appearance when the viewing angle is changed.

Color-only Trademarks

Color-only trademarks consist of only single or multiple color combinations.

Position Trademarks

Position trademarks are defined by the specific position of the logo or the figure on the product.

Special Collective Trademarks for Geographical Names

Industrial business cooperative associations can register using this system, and only the association members can use such trademarks.The trademark must already be well known among consumers. For example, "Imabari Towel" etc.

Defensive Trademarks

The owner of the right can register the same trademark for non-similar goods or services as a "defensive trademark" when the registered trademark is well known among consumers and confusion might occur. Therefore, the owner of the right can prevent other parties registering the same trademark for non-similar goods or services.

商標権 (3) / Trademark (3)

日本国特許庁により様々な商標が登録されています
Various trademarks are registered by the Japan Patent Office (JPO)

音商標は、インターネット上の公報から音を再生することができます
Sound trademarks can be heard in the Official Gazette on the internet
No. は日本の商標登録番号です
"No." is the Japanese trademark registration number

No.5272518
立体商標 / 3D Trademark
株式会社ファミリーマート
Family Mart Co., Ltd.
衣料品・飲食料品など小売等
Clothing items, food and drink, retail, etc.

No.6034112
位置商標 / Position Trademark
日清食品ホールディング
NISSIN FOODS HOLDINGS CO., LTD.
カップ入りの具およびスープ付きの即席麺など
Instant noodles in a cup, etc.

No.4575560
キューピー株式会社
Kewpie Corporation
調味料など
Souce, etc.

No.5930334
色彩のみからなる商標 / Color-only Trademark
株式会社トンボ鉛筆
Tombow Pencil Co., Ltd.
消しゴム
Eraser

No.5842092
音商標 / Sound Trademark
ライオン株式会社
Lion Corporation
石鹸、ウエットティッシュなど
Soap, wet tissues, etc.

No. 5807881
株式会社エドウィン
EDWIN CORPORATION
ズボンなど
Pants, etc.

グーグル エルエルシー
Google LLC
コンピュータソフトウエアなど
Computer software, etc.

No.6062190

これらの図はすべての図からの抜粋です / These figures are excerpted from all figures

ザ・コカ・コーラ カンパニー
The Coca-Cola Company
清涼飲料、コーラ飲料など
Soda, Coke, etc.

No.1499892

No.1610616

No.5225619
立体商標 / 3D Trademark

株式会社サンリオ
SANRIO
文具類など
Stationery, etc.

No.5326862

No.5338414

No.5313632

同じまたは類似する商標でも、指定商品・役務が非類似であれば、別商標として登録されます。以下は、商標「CROWN」「クラウン」が異なる指定商品「自動車」「印刷物」「乳製品」で別の権利者により登録されている例です。

If the designated goods or services are not similar, each trademark is registered even when they are the same. Under the examples, the trademark "CROWN" is registered by different owners for goods which are designated as being different. Goods are cars, printed materials, and milk.

CROWN	No.926786	トヨタ自動車株式会社 / TOYOTA MOTOR CORPORATION 自動車 など / Cars, etc.
CROWN	No.663091	株式会社三省堂 / SANSEIDO 印刷物など / Printed materials, etc.
クラウン	No.1242626	協同乳業株式会社 / KYODO MILK INDUSTRY Co., Ltd. 乳製品、乳清飲料 / Milk and milk products

権利は誰のもの?

基本原則

知的創作物を保護する著作権法、特許法、実用新案法、意匠法において、原則、権利は創作者(著作者、発明者など)に帰属します。例えば著作権法においては著作物を創作する著作者が権利を享有することが規定されています。特許法では「特許を受ける権利」[*1] は発明者に帰属し、「特許を受ける権利」を持たないものが行った出願は、冒認出願であるとして特許権を取得することはできません。実用新案法、意匠法も特許法と同様です。

職務著作・職務発明

ただし、著作権における職務上作成する著作物、並びに特許法における職務発明(実用新案法、意匠法も同様)については、別途それぞれに規定があり、規定条件を満たすものは、その法人または使用者に権利が帰属します。

著作権(職務著作)

法人または使用者が著作物の最初の著作者になるためには、次の2つの条件が満たされなければなりません:
・職務上、著作者である従業員が、使用者の指示により著作物を作成する場合。
・法人または使用者が、法人または使用者の著作物として公表する場合[*2]。

特許権(職務発明) / 実用新案権 / 意匠権

特許法において、従業者等が行った職務発明については、契約、勤務規則その他の定めにおいてあらかじめ使用者等に特許を受ける権利を取得させることを定めたときは、その特許を受ける権利は、その発生した時から当該使用者等に帰属します。発明者は、経済的利益を伴う相当の対価を使用者などへを請求することができます。
この規定内容は、実用新案権、意匠権も 同じです。

[*1] 特許を受ける権利とは、特許出願することのできる権利です。
[*2] コンピュータープログラムについては、この条件は不要です。

Who owns the creation?

Basic Principles

These Acts protect intellectual creations: Copyright Act, Patent Act, Utility Model Act, and Design Act.

The author is the owner of their written creations under the Copyright Act. The inventor has the "right to obtain a patent"[1] under the Patent Act. It is impossible to get an approval from the application if the applicant does not have this right. Utility Model Act and Design Act follow the same rule.

Employee's creation / Employee's invention

There is a separate provision in the Copyright Act, Patent Act, Utility Model Act and Design Act concerning the work produced by an employee during their work duties. Depending on the conditions, the right may belong either to the company or to the employer.

Copyright (employee's creation)

In order for a company to be the initial owner of the creation, the two conditions below must be met :
· The author is an employee and they create the written work, as part of their job responsibilities,at the request of their company or employer.
· The company has to publish the creation and then the company ownership of the right is made public by the company or by the employer[2].

Patents (employee's invention) / Utility Model Rights / Design Rights

If an employee creates an invention and if it is stated in any agreement, employment regulation or any other stipulation that the right to obtaining the patent for any employee invention belongs to the employer, then the right to obtain a patent belongs to the employer. However, the employee has the right to demand a reward in the form of money, promotion, holidays, etc. This provisions are also the same for Utility Model Act and Design Act.

[1] Right to obtain a patent provides the right to file a patent.
[2] This condition does not apply to computer programs.

第3章

Chapter 3

出願から登録

Application to Registration

出願から登録までの流れ

（日本）

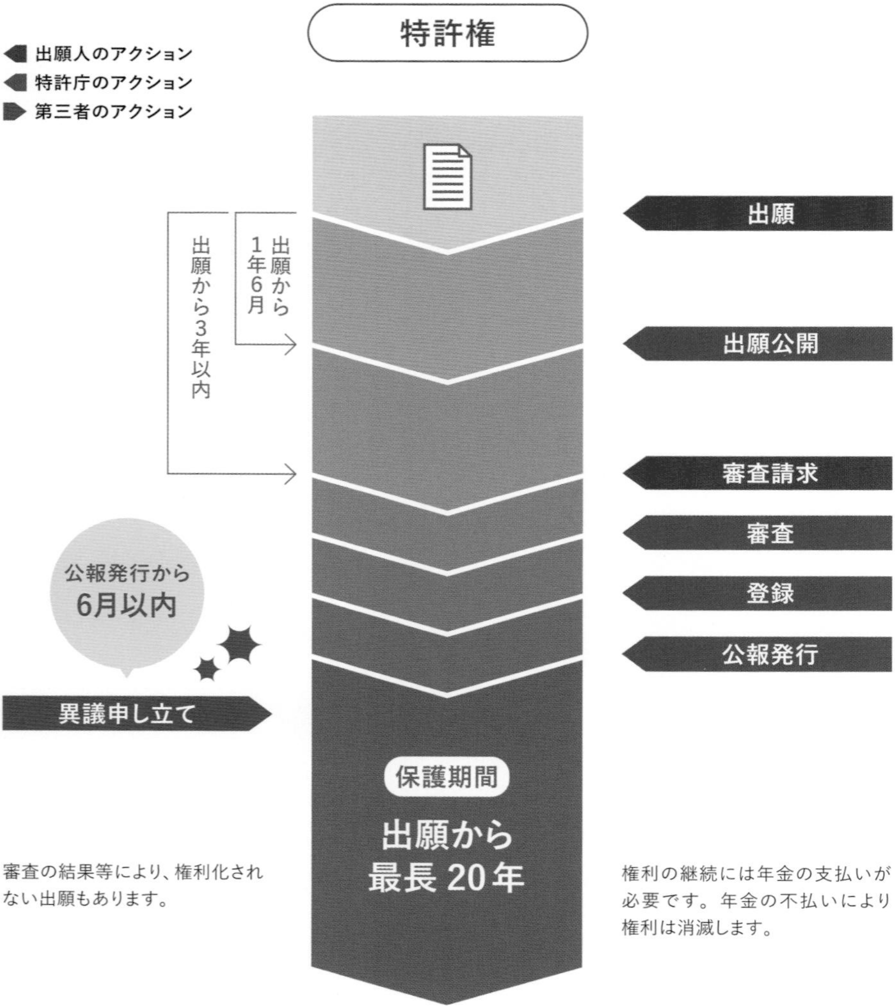

特許権

◀ 出願人のアクション
◀ 特許庁のアクション
▶ 第三者のアクション

出願から3年以内

出願から1年6月

出願

出願公開

審査請求

審査

登録

公報発行

公報発行から
6月以内

異議申し立て

保護期間

出願から
最長 **20年**

審査の結果等により、権利化されない出願もあります。

権利の継続には年金の支払いが必要です。年金の不払いにより権利は消滅します。

From Application to Registration
(Japan)

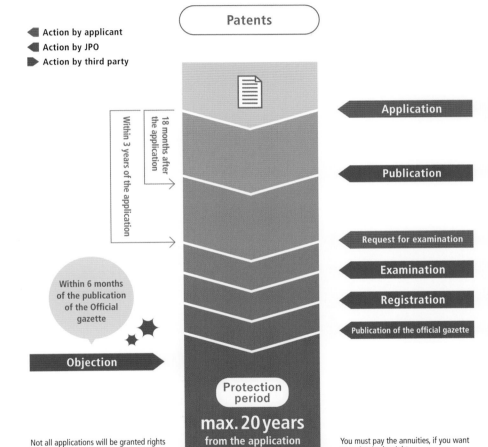

Patents

◀ Action by applicant
◀ Action by JPO
▶ Action by third party

Within 3 years of the application

18 months after the application

Within 6 months of the publication of the Official gazette

Application

Publication

Request for examination

Examination

Registration

Publication of the official gazette

Objection

Protection period

max. 20 years from the application

Not all applications will be granted rights based on factors such as examination or application withdrawal.

You must pay the annuities, if you want to maintain the right.
The right will be withdrawn if you do not pay the annuities.

出願から登録までの流れ
（日本）

実用新案権

◀ 出願人のアクション
◀ 特許庁のアクション

出願

基礎的審査 *

登録

公報発行

権利行使時には
「技術評価書」の
請求が必要

保護期間
出願から
最長 10 年

* 出願の形式的な要件が満たされ
ているかのみ審査が行われます。

権利の継続には年金の支払いが
必要です。年金の不払いにより
権利は消滅します。

From Application to Registration
(Japan)

Utility Model Right

◀ Action by applicant
◀ Action by JPO

Application

Basic examination*

Registration

Publication of the official gazette

It's necessary to acquire a "Technical evaluation document" if youuse the right

Protection period

max. 10 years
from the application

*This examination is only a formality.

You must pay the annuities, if you want to maintain the right.
The right will be withdrawn if you do not pay the annuities.

出願から登録までの流れ
（日本）

意匠権

◀ 出願人のアクション
◀ 特許庁のアクション

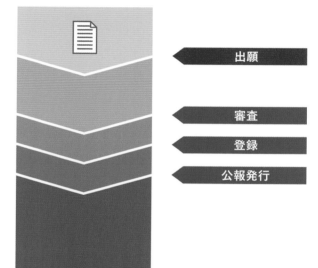

出願

審査

登録

公報発行

保護期間

出願から
最長 25 年

審査の結果等により、権利化されない出願もあります。

権利の継続には年金の支払いが必要です。年金の不払いにより権利は消滅します。

From Application to Registration
(Japan)

Design Rights

◀ Action by applicant
◀ Action by JPO

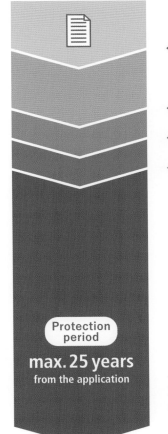

Application

Examination

Registration

Publication of the official gazette

Protection period

max. 25 years
from the application

Not all applications will be granted rights based on factors such as examination or application withdrawal.

You must pay the annuities, if you want to maintain the right.
The right will be withdrawn if you do not pay the annuities.

出願から登録までの流れ

（日本）

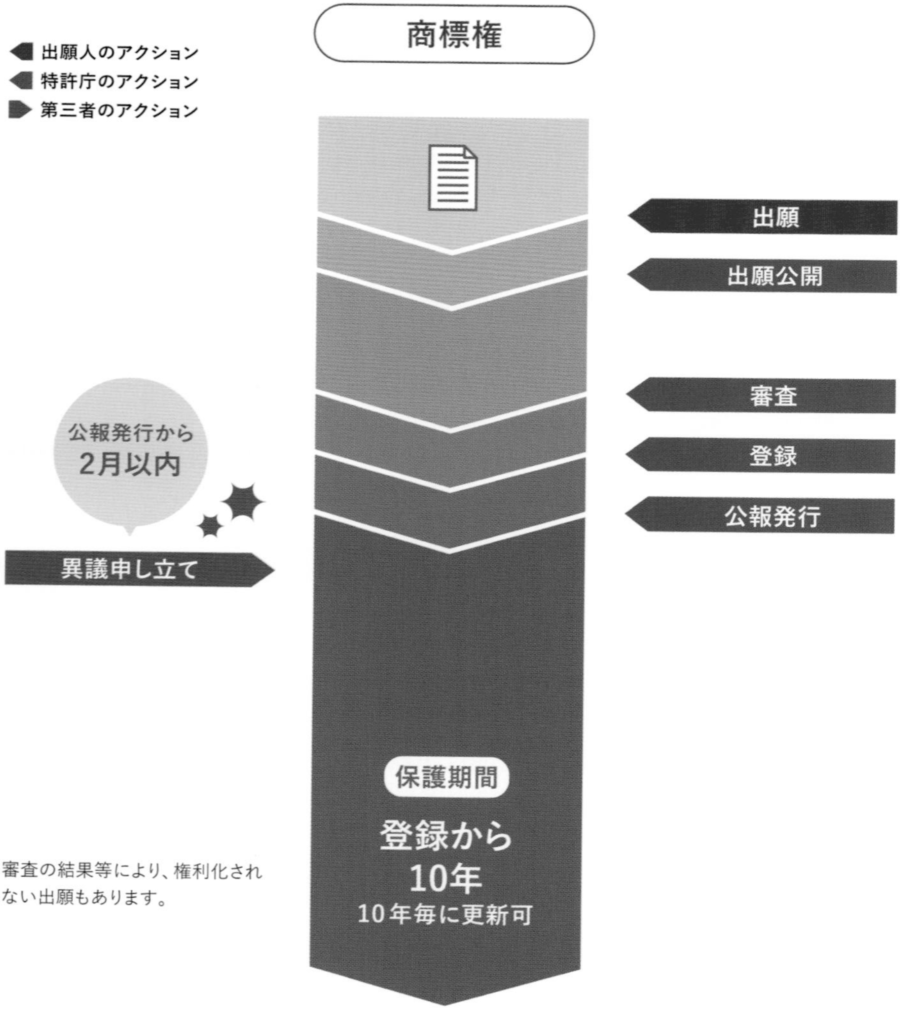

商標権

- ◀ 出願人のアクション
- ◀ 特許庁のアクション
- ▶ 第三者のアクション

出願

出願公開

審査

登録

公報発行

公報発行から
2月以内

異議申し立て

保護期間

登録から
10年
10年毎に更新可

審査の結果等により、権利化され
ない出願もあります。

From Application to Registration
(Japan)

Trademarks

◀ Action by applicant
◀ Action by JPO
▶ Action by third party

Application

Publication

Examination

Registration

Publication of the official gazette

Within 2 months from the publication of the Official gazette

Objection

Protection period

10 years
from the registration
Renewal every 10 years

Not all applications will be granted rights based on factors such as examination or application withdrawal.

保護期間

Protection Period

保護期間
（日本）

	保護期間 （年）	権利起算日	出願／登録／ 年金の支払 または更新	審査 （新規性等）
著作権	70	著作者の死亡日 または公表日(1)	不要	不要
官庁 URL		文化庁　http://www.bunka.go.jp		
特許権	20*	出願日(2)	必要	必要
実用新案権	10*	出願日(3)	必要	不要
意匠権	25*	出願日(4)	必要	必要
商標権	10 更新可	登録日(5)	必要	必要
官庁 URL		日本国特許庁　http://www.jpo.go.jp		

* 最長期間

(1) 著作権の保護期間：個人の著作物は、創作の完成時から著作者の死後70年です。法人著作物は公表日から70年です。米国とEUも同じです。
(2) 特許の保護期間：登録後、出願日から最長20年です。権利維持には年金の支払いが必要です。
(3) 実用新案権の保護期間：出願日から最長10年です。権利維持には年金の支払いが必要です。
(4) 意匠権の保護期間：登録後、出願日から最長25年です。権利維持には年金の支払いが必要です。
(5) 商標権の保護期間：登録後、登録日から10年です。10年ごとに更新費用を支払い、更新することができます。

Protection Period
(Japan)

	Protection period (Years)	Starting point of the rights	Application / Registration / Payment of Annuities or Renewal	Examination (for Novelty and so on)
Copyright	70	After the date of the author's death or Publication date (1)	Not necessary	Not necessary
Office's URL	Agency for Cultural Affairs http://www.bunka.go.jp/english/			
Patent	20*	Application date (2)	Necessary	Necessary
Utility Model Right	10*	Application date (3)	Necessary	Not necessary
Design Right	25*	Application date (4)	Necessary	Necessary
Trademark	10 Renewal	Registration date (5)	Necessary	Necessary
Office's URL	Japan Patent Office (JPO) http://www.jpo.go.jp			

*Maximum term

(1) Protection period of copyright: Personal works are protected from creation accomplishment date to 70 years after the author's death. Works under the name of a corporate body are protected 70 years from the publication date. These are the same in USA and EU.
(2) Protection period of patents: After being granted and max. 20 years from the application date. Annuity payment necessary.
(3) Protection period of utility model rights: Max.10 years from the application date. Annuity payment necessary.
(4) Protection period of design rights: After being granted and max. 25 years from the application date. Annuity payment necessary.
(5) Protection period of trademarks: After being granted and 10 years from the registration date. Renewal possible every 10 years with the renewal fee.

保護期間
(米国)

	保護期間 (年)	権利起算日	出願 / 登録 / 年金の支払 または更新	審査 (新規性等)
著作権	70	著作者の死亡日または 公表日(1)	不要	不要
官庁 URL	米国著作権庁　https://www.copyright.gov			
特許権(2)	20*	出願日(3)	必要	必要
デザインパテント(4)	15	登録日(5)	必要	必要
商標権	10 更新可	登録日(6)	必要	必要
官庁 URL	米国特許商標庁　http://uspto.gov			

* 最長期間

(1) 著作権の保護期間: 日本と同じです。
(2) 米国には実用新案法はなく、技術的創作は特許で保護されます。
(3) 特許権の保護期間: 日本と同じです。
(4) 米国では、意匠は特許法に規定されており、デザインパテントと呼ばれます。
(5) デザインパテントの保護期間: 登録後、登録日から15年です。権利化後の年金の支払いはありません。
(6) 商標権の保護期間: 日本と同じです。ただし、米国内における使用が必要です。

Protection Period
(USA)

	Protection period (Years)	Starting point of the rights	Application / Registration / Payment of Annuities or Renewal	Examination (for Novelty and so on)
Copyright	70	After the date of the author's death or Publication date (1)	Not necessary	Not necessary
Office's URL	US Copyright Office https://www.copyright.gov			
Patent (2)	20*	Application date (3)	Necessary	Necessary
Design Patent (4)	15	Registration date (5)	Necessary	Not necessary
Trademark	10 Renewal	Registration date (6)	Necessary	Necessary
Office's URL	United States Patent and Trademark Office (USPTO) http://uspto.gov			

*Maximum term

(1) Protection period of opyright: Same as Japan.
(2) There is no Utility Model Act, inventions are protected by Patent Act.
(3) Protection period of patents: Same as Japan.
(4) In USA, designs are defined under Patent Act, called design patent.
(5) Protection period of design patent: After being granted and 15 years from the registration date. Annuity payment not necessary.
(6) Protection period of trademarks: Use of trademark is required.

保護期間
(EU)

	保護期間 （年）	権利起算日	出願／登録／ 年金の支払 または更新	審査 （新規性等）
著作権	70	著作者の死亡日または 公表日(1)	不要	不要
官庁 URL	欧州連合　https://europa.eu			
特許権	20*	出願日(2)	必要	必要
Office's URL	欧州特許庁　https://www.epo.org/index.html			
意匠権(3) （RCD）	25*	出願日(4)	必要	不要
商標権	10 更新可	出願日(2)	必要	必要
官庁 URL	欧州連合知的財産庁　https://euipo.europa.eu/			

* 最長期間

・欧州連合(EU)では、加盟国内をカバーする統一法(EU規則、ヨーロッパ特許条約、EU統一意匠法、EU統一商標法)があります。これらの法律は、各国内法と共存しています。
・欧州特許庁(EPO)は特許を扱っており、登録された特許は欧州特許と呼ばれます。
・欧州連合知的財産庁(EUIPO)は意匠(コミュニティーデザイン)と商標を扱っています。
(1)著作権の保護期間：日本と同じです。
(2)特許・商標の保護期間：日本と同じです。
(3)意匠権は 2 種あり、官庁への出願・登録を必要とする登録意匠権(RCD)と、これらの手続きが不要な非登録意匠権(UCD)です。
(4)RCDの保護期間：出願日から 5 年毎の更新により、最長 25 年です。更新費用の支払いが必要です。UCD の保護期間：EU域内で販売開始または公開された日から3年です。

Protection Period
(EU)

	Protection period (Years)	Starting point of the rights	Application / Registration / Payment of Annuities or Renewal	Examination (for Novelty and so on)
Copyright	70	After the date of the author's death or Publication date (1)	Not necessary	Not necessary
Office's URL	European union　https://europa.eu			
Patent	20*	Application date (2)	Necessary	Necessary
Office's URL	European Patent Office (EPO)　https://www.epo.org/index.html			
Design right (3) (RCD)	25*	Application date (4)	Necessary	Not necessary
Trademark	10 Renewal	Application date (2)	Necessary	Necessary
Office's URL	European IP Office (EUIPO)　https://euipo.europa.eu/			

*Maximum term

· The European Union (EU) has unified laws (European Union Directive (including Copyright),
 European Patent Convention, Community design, EU trademark), which cover EU member countries.
 These laws coexist with national laws.
· European Patent office (EPO) deals with patents, called European patents.
· European Union IP Office (EUIPO) deals with design rights (community design) and trademarks.
(1) Protection period of copyright: Same as Japan.
(2) Protection period of patents, trademark: Same as Japan.
(3) There are two types of design rights, Registered Community Designs (RCD) and Unregistered Community
 Designs (UCD). RCD requires application and registration by EUIPO. Not required by UCD.
(4) Protection period of RCD: 5 years from the application date, renewal possible every 5 years up to maximum 25
 years. Renewal payment necessary. Protection period of UCD: 3 years from entering the EU market.

保護期間
（中国）

	保護期間 （年）	権利起算日	出願／登録／ 年金の支払 または更新	審査 （新規性等）
著作権	50	著作者の死亡日または 公表日(1)	不要	不要
官庁 URL	国家版権局　http://www.ncac.gov.cn			
特許権	20*	出願日(3)	必要	必要
実用新案権(2)	10*	出願日(4)	必要	不要
意匠特許権(2)	10*	出願日(4)	必要	不要
商標権	10 更新可	出願日(3)	必要	必要
官庁 URL	国家知識産権局　http://english.cnipa.gov.cn/			

＊最長期間

(1) 著作権の保護期間は、個人の著作物は、創作の完成時から著作者の死後 50 年、法人著作物は公表
　　後 50 年です。
(2) 中国では、実用新案権と意匠権は特許法に規定されています。
(3) 特許・商標の保護期間：日本と同じです。
(4) 実用新案権・意匠特許権の保護期間：出願日から最長 10 年です。権利維持には年金の支払いが
　　必要です。

Protection Period
(China)

	Protection period (Years)	Starting point of the rights	Application / Registration / Payment of Annuities or Renewal	Examination (for Novelty and so on)
Copyright	50	After the date of the author's death or Publication date (1)	Not necessary	Not necessary
Office's URL	National Copyright Administration of China (NCAC)　http://www.ncac.gov.cn			
Patent	20*	Application date (3)	Necessary	Necessary
Utility Model Rights (2)	10*	Application date (4)	Necessary	Not necessary
Design Patent (2)	10*	Application date (4)	Necessary	Not necessary
Trademark	10 Renewal	Application date (3)	Necessary	Necessary
Office's URL	National Intellectual Property Administration, PRC (CNIPA)　http://english.cnipa.gov.cn/			

*Maximum term

(1) Protection period of copyright: Personal works are protected from creation accomplishment date to 50 years after the author's death. Works under the name of a corporate body are protected 50 years from the publication.
(2) Utility model rights and design rights are covered under the Patent Act.
(3) Protection period of patents / trademarks: Same as Japan.
(4) Protection period of utility model rights / design patents: 10 years from the application date. Annuity payment necessary.

第5章

Chapter 5

国 際 出 願

International Application

世界知的所有権機構
(WIPO)

WIPO は、知的財産に関するサービス、政策、情報および協力に関する世界的なフォーラムで、国連の専門機関として、現在 192 の国が加盟しています。その使命は、すべての人の利益のために革新と創造性を可能にする、バランスのとれた効果的な国際知的財産（IP）システムを導き、そして開発することです。 WIPO は 1967 年に設立され、彼らの権限、統治機関および手続きについて WIPO 条約＊により規定されています。

主な条約

パリ条約（締約国：177）

パリ条約は 1883 年に採択され、最も広い意味で産業財産権に適用されています。
特許、商標、産業デザイン、実用新案、サービスマーク、商号、地理的表示、および不正競争の抑止が含まれています。この合意は、クリエイターにとって、自身の知的創作が他国においても確実に保護されることを手助けする、最初の大きなステップでした（70ページ参照）。

ベルヌ条約（締約国：176）

ベルヌ条約は 1886 年に採択され、作品の保護とその著作者の権利を扱っています。
作家、ミュージシャン、詩人、画家などのクリエイターに、自身の作品の使用方法、使用者、使用期間をコントロールする手段を提供しています。 それは以下の 3 つの基本原則に基づいています。

・締約国間において、締約国の著作者における創作、または最初に締約国において公開された著作物は、他の締約国においても同様の保護が与えられる。
・原則、自動的に保護される。
・原則、保護は国ごとに独立していること。

また、与えられるべき最低限の保護に関する規定、およびそれらを使用することを望む途上国が利用可能な特別規定を含んでいます。

＊世界知的所有権機関を設立する条約

World Intellectual Property Organization
(WIPO)

WIPO is the global forum for intellectual property services, policy, information and cooperation. It is a specialized agency of the United Nations, currently with 192 member states. Its mission is to lead and develop a balanced and effective international IP system that allows innovation and creativity for the benefit of all. Their mandate, governing bodies and procedures are laid out in the WIPO Convention*, which marked the establishment of WIPO in 1967.

The main conventions

Paris Convention (Contracting Parties: 177)
The Paris Convention was adopted in 1883, and it applies to industrial property rights in the broadest sense. It covers patents, trademarks, industrial designs, utility models, service marks, trade names, geographical indications, and the repression of unfair competition. This agreement was the first major step taken to help creators ensure that their intellectual works were protected in other countries (see page 70).

Berne Convention (Contracting Parties: 176)
The Berne Convention was adopted in 1886, deals with the protection of works and the rights of their authors. It provides creators, such as authors, musicians, poets and painters, means to control how, by whom and on what terms their work are used. It is based on three basic principles:

- Works originating in one of the contracting states (works from the same origin as the author or first published in that country) must be given the same protection in each contracting state.
- Principle of "automatic" protection.
- Principle of "independence" of protection.

It also contains provisions which determine the minimum protection to be granted, as well as special provisions available to less-developed countries that wish to use them.

* Convention Establishing the World Intellectual Property Organization

外国への出願

同じ内容の出願を外国へも出願する時に活用することのできる制度があります。

パリ条約＊における優先権制度

産業財産権である、特許権、実用新案権、意匠権、商標権は、各国官庁へ出願、登録することにより、当該官庁国において権利が発生します（属地主義）。複数国において同時に出願、登録手続を行うことは出願人に大きな負担となるため、その軽減措置としてパリ条約における優先権の制度があります。この制度は、締約国おいて最初に特許、実用新案、意匠、もしくは商標の出願をした者は、他の締約国において同内容の出願をする際、以下の期間中優先権を主張することにより、新規性、進歩性などの判断について、最初に出願した国の出願日に出願したものとして扱われる効果を得ることができます。

優先期間
特許権 / 実用新権　：最初の出願日（第1国出願日）から 1 年
意匠権 / 商標権　　：最初の出願日（第1国出願日）から 6 月

国際出願・登録制度

上記のように、複数国への出願・登録に対する出願人負担軽減のため、特許権、意匠権、商標権にはWIPO が提供する国際出願・登録制度があり、各制度の締約国は当該制度を活用することができます（72 ページ参照）。

外国官庁に対する手続きは、原則現地代理人による手続きが必要です。
＊パリ条約の概要　https://www.wipo.int/treaties/en/ip/paris/summary_paris.html

IP Applications in other Countries

There are systems that applicants can utilize when they file the same application in other countries.

Priority System under the Paris Convention*

In principle, industrial property rights (patents, utility model rights, design rights and trademarks) are filed and registered with each of the national government offices (territoriality). Since it is a heavy burden to make the application and the registration in multiple countries, there is one mitigation measure from the Paris Convention called priority. The priority system means that, on the basis of a first application filed in one of the contracting states, the applicant may, within a certain period of time, apply for protection with priority in any of the other contracting states. Regarding the examination about novelty, or invention step and etc., these subsequent applications will be regarded as if they had been filed on the same day as the first application. In other words, they will have priority over applications filed by others during the said period of time for the same invention, utility model, industrial design or trademark.

Period of Time for the Priority
Patents / Utility Model rights   : From the first application date to 1 year
Design rights / Trademarks…   : From the first application date to 6 months

---

International Application / Registration Systems

As mentioned above, in order to reduce the burden on applicants for application and registration for multiple countries, there are international application / registration systems that WIPO provides for patents, design rights and trademarks. Contracting countries' applicants can utilize these systems (see 73 page).

When dealing in a foreign country's office, local legal representation is essential.
* Summary of the Paris Convention   https://www.wipo.int/treaties/en/ip/paris/summary_paris.html

国際出願・登録制度

WIPOは、特許、工業意匠、商標の国際出願登録システムを提供しており、申請者はWIPO国際事務局へ行う一つの出願で複数の国で出願登録することができます。WIPOでは審査は行わず、出願人が指定した各国で審査は行われます。各システムの内容、プロセス、および締約国はそれぞれ異なり、その数も年々増加しています。そのため、各システムを利用する際には、まず加盟国を確認することが必要です。

PCT: 国際特許システム（締約国: 153）

特許協力条約（PCT）は、出願人が発明について国際的に特許保護を求める際に利用することのできるシステムです。PCTの下で単一の国際特許出願を行うことにより、出願人は同時にすべての加盟国へ出願したことと同等の効果を得ることができます。しかし、基本的に出願から30月以内に、出願人は保護を必要とする個々の国々の官庁へ申請手続きを行う（国内段階への移行）必要があり、審査は各国で行われます。

ハーグ：国際デザインシステム（90の国をカバー）

工業意匠の国際登録のためのハーグシステムは、単一の国際出願の提出によって最大100の意匠を登録するための実用的なビジネスソリューションを提供しています。この制度の下では、WIPOに対し費用を含めた単一の出願手続きを行い、保護を求める国を指定します。審査は各国で行われます。ハーグシステムは、2つの国際条約（ジュネーブアクト: 1999年アクト、ハーグアクト: 1960年アクト）で構成されています。日本はジュネーブアクト（締約国: 63）に加盟しています。同一のアクトに加盟している国間でその国際システムを活用することができます。

マドリッド: 国際商標システム（122の国をカバー）

マドリッドシステムでは、WIPOに対し費用を含めた単一の出願手続きを行い、保護を求める国を指定します。出願人はこのシステムを通して世界的な商標ポートフォリオを更新または拡大することができます。審査は各国で行われます。マドリッドシステムは、2種の異なる法律（アクト）を有し、日本はマドリッドプロトコル（締約国: 104）に加盟しています。この制度を利用するには、まず自国で基礎となる出願または登録が必要です。

締約国には、政府間機関（IGO）も含まれます。

International Applications and Registration Systems

WIPO provides systems for international applications and registrations of patents, industrial designs, and trademarks, allowing applicants to file and register in multiple countries through a single application to WIPO. WIPO does not conduct examination, the offices of the designated countries by applicant, conduct examination. The structure, process and membership of each system below may vary. However, the number of the member countries using these systems is increasing. Therefore, it is vital to check the member countries when using each of WIPO's systems.

PCT: International Patent System (Contracting states: 153)

The system of the Patent Cooperation Treaty (PCT) assists applicants when seeking international patent protection for their inventions. It helps Patent Offices with their patent granting decisions and provides public access to extensive technical information regarding past applications. By filing one international patent application under the PCT, applicants can simultaneously seek protection for an invention in all member countries. However, the applicant must transfer the application into the national phase basically within 30 months from the application (choose the countries that they will apply for). Examination will be conducted country by country.

HAGUE: International Design System (Covering 90 countries)

The Hague System for the international registration of industrial designs provides a practical business solution for registering up to 100 designs through the filing of one single international application. Under this system it is possible to file a single application and pay one set of fees to apply for protection in multiple contracting countries. The examination is held in each country. The Hague System is constituted by two international treaties which are Geneva Act (1999 Act) and Hague Act (1960 Act). Japan has joined Geneva Act (contracting parties: 63). The international system can be used between countries participating in the same act.

MADRID: International Trademark System (Covering 122 countries)

The Madrid System is possible to file a single application and pay one set of fees to apply for protection in multiple contracting countries. Examinations are held in each country that you wish to register in. You can renew or expand your global Trademark portfolio through one centralized system. The Madrid System has 2 Acts. Japan has been joined Madrid Protocol (contracting parties: 104). Between countries contracted same Act, they can utilize the international system. At first, a basic application or registration is necessary in your own country when using this system.

The countries are including Intergovernmental organization (IGO).

国際出願・登録制度

（出願から権利化までの流れ）

PCT / 特許権

国際段階

国際事務局

国際出願

国際調査 / 見解書

国際公開

国内段階　出願人により各国へ移行

各国（政府間機関含む）官庁

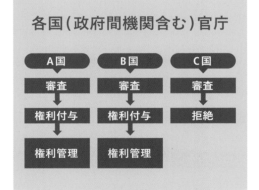

A国	B国	C国
審査	審査	審査
権利付与	権利付与	拒絶
権利管理	権利管理	

各国で行われる審査により拒絶されることがあります。

International Application and Registration System
(Application to Grant of the right)

PCT / Patents

International phase

WIPO office

International Application

↓

International Search Report with Opinion

↓

International Publication

National phase: transfer to each county's office by applicant

Each country's office (including IGO)

Country A	Country B	Country C
Examination	Examination	Examination
Grant of the right	Grant of the right	Refusal of protection
Management of the right	Management of the right	

Not all applications will be granted rights based on factors such as examination.

国際出願・登録制度

（出願から権利化までの流れ）

ハーグ / 意匠権

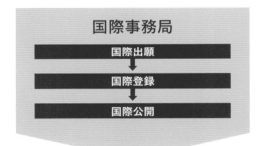

新規性などの実体審査
を行わない国もあります

各国で行われる審査に
より拒絶されることがあ
ります。

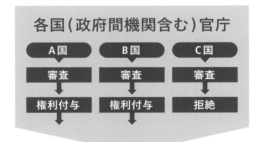

権利は国際事務局で一元管理されます。

International Application and Registration System
(Application to Grant of the right)

HAGUE / Design rights

WIPO office

International Application
↓
International Registration
↓
International Publication

Each country's office (including IGO)

Country A	Country B	Country C
↓	↓	↓
Examination	Examination	Examination
↓	↓	↓
Grant of the right	Grant of the right	Refusal of protection

Some countries don't examine novelty and so on.

Not all applications will be granted rights based on factors such as examination.

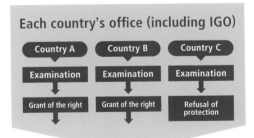

WIPO office

Management of the right

Renewal every 5 years / Max. years by each country's law

Design rights are managed by WIPO office.

国際出願・登録制度
（出願から権利化までの流れ）

マドリッド / 商標権

自国官庁

国際出願には基礎出願または基礎登録が必要です。

基礎出願、基礎登録

権利管理

国際事務局

国際出願

国際登録

国際公開

各国（政府間機関含む）官庁

A国	B国	C国
審査	審査	審査
権利付与	権利付与	拒絶

各国で行われる審査により拒絶されることがあります。

国際事務局

権利管理

10年毎に更新可能

権利は国際事務局で一元管理されます。

International Application and Registration System
(Application to Grant of the right)

MADRID / Trademarks

Own country's office

International application requires the basic application or basic registration.

Basic application or Basic registration

Maintenance of the right

WIPO office

International Application

↓

International Registration

↓

International Publication

Each country's office (including IGO)

Country A | Country B | Country C

Examination | Examination | Examination

Grant of the right | Grant of the right | Refusal of protection

Not all applications will be granted rights based on factors such as examination.

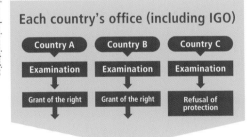

WIPO office

Management of the right

Renewal every 10 years

Trademarks are managed by WIPO office.

第6章

Chapter 6

その他

Other Issues

権利調査

特許権、意匠権、商標権などの産業財産権は、故意、過失を問わず権利侵害が成立します。他者の権利を侵害しないためには、製品の製造や販売、サービスの実施、商標の使用を開始する前に、既に成立している権利、および出願中のものについて調査を行うことが必須です。また、現在は商品やサービスの企画の段階から権利調査を行うことが常套化しています。商品化が進んだ段階で他者の権利を発見し、変更や中止を避ける狙いがあります。権利は国ごとに成立するため、国際的なビジネスを行う際は、グローバルな調査が必要になります。日本とWIPOのデータベースは、以下のURLからアクセスできます。

日本のデータベース

J-PlatPat（特許情報プラットフォーム）　　　　https://www.j-platpat.inpit.go.jp

このデータベースから、日本で出願、登録された特許権、実用新案権、意匠権、商標権を調査することができます。また、一部外国公報の検索もできます。出願公開制度のある特許と商標は、登録までの進捗状況など、経過情報を確認することもできます。

WIPOのデータベース

法域によりデータベースが分かれています。多くの国の権利情報を同時に検索することができます。

特許権	パテントスコープ	日本語での検索が可能
PATENTSCOPE	https://patentscope2.wipo.int/search/ja/search.jsf	
意匠権	グローバルデザイン データベース	
Global Design Database	https://www.wipo.int/designdb/en	
商標権	グローバルブランド データベース	
Global Brand Database	http://www.wipo.int/branddb/en	

IP Rights Search Resources

Infringement of industrial property rights (patents, design rights, trademarks) happens regardless of whether the violation was intentional or not. In order to avoid infringing on the rights of others, it is imperative to search registered rights and pending applications before starting a new product or service. For products and services, it is a common procedure to search IP rights from early planning stages, in order to find conflicting rights and avoid changes / cancellations at later stages. If you are doing business internationally then it is imperative to thoroughly search rights in your target country's market. Databases of Japan and WIPO can be accessed at the following URLs.

Japanese database

J-PlatPat (Japan Platform for Patent Information)   https://www.j-platpat.inpit.go.jp

It is possible to search for patents, utility model rights, design rights, trademarks which are filed and registered in Japan and in some other countries. Patents and trademarks which have been published prior to registration can also have their application progress and their rights checked.

WIPO's database

The database is divided into Patents, Design rights (industrial designs), and Trademarks. You can search the rights in multiple countries simultaneously.

Patents   PATENTSCOPE

https://patentscope2.wipo.int/search/ja/search.jsf

Design rights   Global Design Database

https://www.wipo.int/designdb/en

Trademarks   Global Brand Database

http://www.wipo.int/branddb/en

地理的表示
(GI)

日本にも多くの産地と結びついた高品質の農林水産物などがあり、それらはそのブランド名と共に広く知られています。これらを保護するために地理的表示の保護制度があります。登録はその生産地や品質の基準を農林水産大臣へ申請して行います。登録内容を満たす産品は「地理的表示」を使用することができ、かつ下記のGIマークを使用することができます。いったん登録されると登録が取り消されない限りは存続し、更新手続きは不要です。これにより、その産品が満たすべき品質の基準も登録されるため、産品の品質の統一化が図られ、高品質な農林水産物の更なる発展を奨励し、消費者への信頼を得ることができます。また、違反品に対しては行政による保護が図られます。例えば、以下のような産品が登録されています。

地理的表示の名称	区分	生産地域
青森カシス	果実類 すぐり類	青森県青森市など
神戸ビーフ	生鮮肉類 牛肉	兵庫県内
夕張メロン	野菜類 メロン	北海道夕張市
三輪素麺	穀物類加工品類 そうめん類	奈良県全域

GI マーク

登録されている地理的表示 (GI) 品は、以下の URL から検索することができます。
GI品の検索　https://gi-act.maff.go.jp/

地理的表示に関する農林水産省HP
http://www.maff.go.jp/j/shokusan/gi_act/index.html

・国際的には、いくつかの国際条約 [WIPO、及び世界貿易機関 (WTO) による知的財産権の貿易関連の側面に関する協定 (TRIPS) によって管理されているものを含む] により地理的表示または原産地名称の保護を部分的または全体的に扱っています。
・日本とEU間では、EPA (Economic Partnership Agreement) の発効により、各指定されたGI品目について、相互に高いレベルでの保護が強化されることになりました。

Geographical Indications
(GI)

In Japan, there are many high-quality regional-brand products which have obtained a good reputation, as a result of unique production methods and the natural characteristics of the production area (such as climate and soil conditions). The GI Act therefore provides a system where the government registers the names of such products through application. Once registered, a renewal procedure is unnecessary unless the registration is canceled. The GI Act protects the interests of producers through the establishment of the GI protection system, thereby contributing to the development of the agricultural, forestry, and fishery industries as well as protecting the interests of the consumers. For example, the products below are registered under the GI Act.

Name of GI	Class	Production Area
Aomori cassis	Fruit	Aomori Prefecture
Kobe Beef	Meat	Hyogo Prefecture
Yubari Melon	Vegetable	Yubari city, Hokkaido
Miwa Soumen	Processed Foodstuffs	Nara Prefecture

GI Mark

You can search the registered GI products on the internet.
https://gi-act.maff.go.jp/en/register/

Information about GI, provided by MAFF (Ministry of Agriculture, Forestry and Fisheries)
http://www.maff.go.jp/e/policies/intel/gi_act/index.html

· Worldwide, a number of treaties deal partly or entirely with the protection of geographical indications or appellations of origin, including those administered by WIPO and the World Trade Organization's (WTO) Agreement on Trade Related Aspects of Intellectual Property Rights (TRIPS).
· Between Japan and the EU, under the EPA (Economic Partnership Agreement), mutual high-level protection is strengthened for each GI product.

不正競争防止法

日本の不正競争防止法は、事業者間の営業上の利益および公正な競争の確保を図るための法律です。定義において複数の項目を不正競争行為として規定し、それに該当した場合、相手方に対し知的財産権同様に、差止請求および損害賠償などの請求をすることができます。不正競争行為の中には、特許権、意匠権、商標権に関連する行為も含まれており、違法行為に対し、これらの権利と共に不正競争防止法違反として知的財産を保護することができます。ただし、譲渡やライセンスをすることのできる権利は発生しません。不正競争行為が発生した時点の状況で違法か否かが判断されます。

不正競争防止法で規定されている主な不正競争行為

(1) 他人の周知な表示と同一または類似の表示を使用した商品を複製などして他人の商品との混同を起こさせるような行為
(2) 自己の商品等表示として、他人の著名な表示を使用した商品を譲渡などする行為
(3) 他人の商品の形態を模倣した商品を提供する行為*
(4) 営業秘密に関する不正行為
(5) コピーガードなどを解除する装置などを提供する行為
(6) ドメイン名に関する不正行為
(7) 原産地や品質などの虚偽表示行為
(8) 競争関係にある他人の信用を傷つける虚偽の事実を流布する行為
(9) 外国の国旗や紋章などの不正使用行為
(10) 外国の公務員に対する賄賂に関する行為

不正競争防止法に関する経済産業省HP
http://www.meti.go.jp/policy/economy/chizai/chiteki

---

* この規定は、商品が最初に販売された日から3年間に限り適用を受けることができます。

Unfair Competition Prevention Act

Japanese Unfair Competition Prevention Act ensures fair competition and helps protect legitimate business activities by defining what is unfair competition: when such infringement occurs, similar to IP rights violation, the infringed party can request an injunction and/or compensation, etc. The Unfair Competition Prevention Act covers a wide range of topics and includes a list of cases related to IP rights, such as patents, design rights and trademarks. Although it can protect IP from acts of infringement, it is not possible to transfer or license any protection because there are no rights under the Unfair Competition Prevention Act. In addition, judgements are made according to specific circumstances at any given time.

Main acts of unfair competition stipulated by the Unfair Competition Prevention Act

(1) Confusing customers by creating a product that duplicates or uses the same or similar publicly known sources and trademarks
(2) Falsely transfer famous names or trademarks to a product as an indication of your own products
(3) Imitating the form of a third party's product*
(4) Leaking confidential sales information
(5) Providing equipment to stop copy guard etc.
(6) Misconduct related to domain names
(7) Mislabeling and causing confusion to customers regarding the quality or source of a product
(8) Dissemination of false allegations that harm the business reputation of other competitors
(9) Improper use of foreign flag or emblem
(10) Bribery of foreign government officials

Information about Unfair Competition Privation Act by METI (Ministry of Economy, Trade and Industry)
http://www.meti.go.jp/policy/economy/chizai/chiteki

* This regulation can be applied for 3 years from the date the product was first sold.

権利侵害

著作権、特許権、実用新案権、意匠権、または商標権を侵害された場合、権利者は自己の権利を侵害する者に対し、主に以下の民事上の請求を行うことができます。また刑事上の罰則規定もあります。不正競争防止法においても同様の規定*が設けられています。地理的表示（GI）は、不正使用に対し行政措置が行われます。不正使用者に対し農林水産大臣による措置命令が行われ、改善されない場合には罰則が科されます。基本的に侵害を主張する側に立証責任があります。

差止請求
権利者は自己の権利を侵害する者または侵害する恐れがある者に対し、その侵害の停止または予防を請求することができます。例えば侵害品に対し、その商品の製造、販売等の中止を請求することができます。

損害賠償請求
権利者は自己の権利を侵害した者に対し、その侵害により自己が受けた損害の賠償を請求することができます。例えば模倣品の出現により売り上げが減少した場合、損害額は、侵害者が侵害行為により得た利益の額などにより算出されます。

水際措置
水際取締まりは、知的財産権侵害品の輸出、または輸入の差止めを税関で行う手続きです。特に模倣品は、中国など海外で製造されるケースが多いので、海外で製造され日本国内で販売される模倣品に対しては、税関での輸入差止、いわゆる水際措置が有効です。関税法に規定された、「輸入してはならない貨物」および「輸出してはならない貨物」の中に知的財産権の侵害物品が含まれています。

* 不正競争行為の中には刑事罰が課されないものもあります。

Infringement of IP Rights

When copyright, patents, utility model rights, design rights or trademarks are violated, right holders usually make the following requests to the violators under civil law. There are also criminal penalties. The same provisions also apply to the Unfair Competition Act*. Geographical indications (GI) are subject to administrative measures against unauthorized use. The Minister of Agriculture, Forestry and Fisheries will issue an order for improper users, who will be punished if the situation is not improved. Basically, the claimant of the infringement has the burden of proof.

Injunction request

A rightsholder may request a person who infringes on their rights (or a person who is likely to infringe) to suspend the product / service, thus preventing a potential violation. For example, a rightsholder can request the suspension of the manufacturing and sales of a product.

Claims for damages

A rightsholder can demand compensation from a violator for loss of profits. For example, if sales decrease due to the appearance of counterfeit goods, the compensation amount is calculated based on the profits obtained by the infringer as a result of the violation.

Import restrictions

A rightsholder can request a customs office to prevent the import and / or export of goods which violate IP rights. A good example of the effectiveness of this measure is when counterfeit goods are manufactured overseas then imported to Japan. These goods that infringe IP rights cannot be imported and exported to the country due to Japanese customs laws.

* Some acts of unfair competition do not impose criminal penalties.

知的財産権 復習

IP Rights Review

事 例 問 題

Case Study

著作物
（著作権の保護対象）

Q1. 日本の著作権法で保護されるものはどれでしょうか？

以下を記載してください。

保護されるもの： ◯　保護されないもの： ✕　どちらもあり得るもの： △

- [ ] 映画
- [ ] 映画の脚本
- [ ] 音楽
- [ ] 振り付け
- [ ] パントマイム
- [ ] 絵画
- [ ] 彫刻

- [ ] 建築物
- [ ] 写真
- [ ] 小説
- [ ] 論文
- [ ] ゲーム
- [ ] 漫画

- [ ] 地図
- [ ] 設計図面
- [ ] 図表
- [ ] 模型
- [ ] 自動車
- [ ] ボールペン
- [ ] アイコン

- [ ] 書体
- [ ] ロゴマーク
- [ ] ブランド名
- [ ] コンピューター プログラム
- [ ] データベース

Objects Protected by Copyright Act

Q1. Which of these are protected under the Copyright Act in Japan?

Please mark according to the condition;

Protected : ◯   Not protected : ✕   Both : △

☐ Movies   ☐ Architecture   ☐ Maps   ☐ Typefaces

☐ Movie scripts   ☐ Photographs   ☐ Design drawings   ☐ Logo marks

☐ Music   ☐ Novels   ☐ Charts   ☐ Brand names

☐ Choreography   ☐ Treatise   ☐ Models   ☐ Computer programs

☐ Pantomime   ☐ Games   ☐ Cars

☐ Paintings   ☐ Cartoons   ☐ Ballpoint pens   ☐ Databases

☐ Sculptures   ☐ Icons

事例問題

Q2-1. これらは知的財産権侵害でしょうか?
侵害の場合、誰が何の権利を侵しているでしょうか?

写真家Aは1月1日に写真を撮影し、3月1日にその写真が雑誌に掲載されました。写真家Bは、1月2日に写真家Aの写真を知らずに、酷似する写真(下図参照)を撮影し、2月1日にその写真をインターネット上に公開しました。

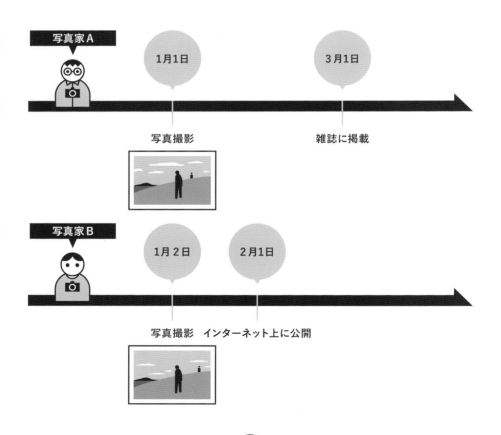

Case study

Q2-1. Considering how similar these two pieces of work are, was there any IP rights infringement in this situation? If so, who is the offender and which rights were violated?

The first picture was taken by Photographer A on January 1st, then it was published in a magazine on March 1st. The second very similar picture (see below the figures) was taken by Photographer B, unfamiliar with photographer A's work, on January 2nd, who then published it online on February 1st.

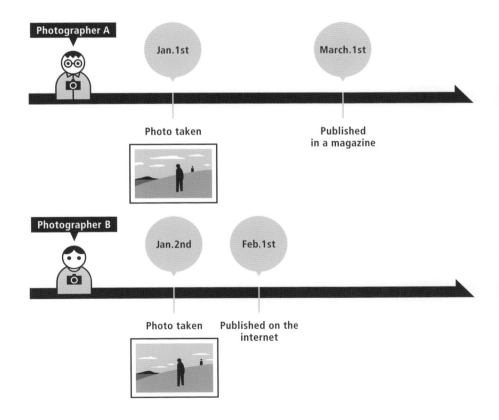

事例問題

Q2-2. これらは知的財産権侵害でしょうか?
侵害の場合、誰が何の権利を侵しているでしょうか?

写真家Aは1月2日に写真を撮影し、2月1日にその写真をインターネット上に公開しました。写真家Bは、3月1日にAの写真に酷似する写真(下図参照)を撮影しました。

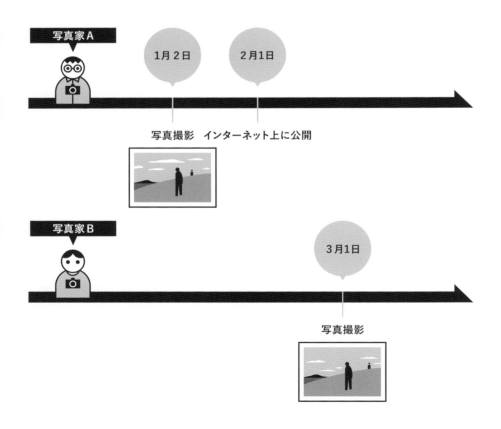

写真家A

1月2日　　　2月1日

写真撮影　インターネット上に公開

写真家B

3月1日

写真撮影

Case study

Q2-2. Considering how similar these two pieces of work are, was there any IP rights infringement in this situation? If so, who is the offender and which rights were violated?

Photographer A took a picture on January 2nd. It was published on the internet on February 1st. Photographer B took a very similar picture (see below the figures) to Photographer A's work on March 1st.

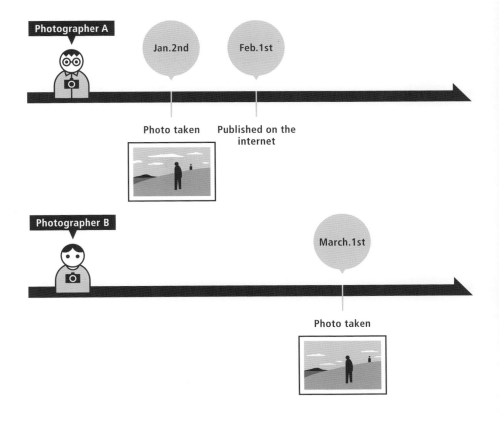

事例問題

Q2-3. これらは知的財産権侵害でしょうか?
侵害の場合、誰が何の権利を侵しているでしょうか?

写真家 A は 1 月 2 日に写真を撮影し、2 月 1 日にその写真をインターネット上に公開しました。写真家 B は 3 月 1 日に酷似する写真（下図参照）を撮影し、4 月 1 日にその写真が雑誌に掲載されました。

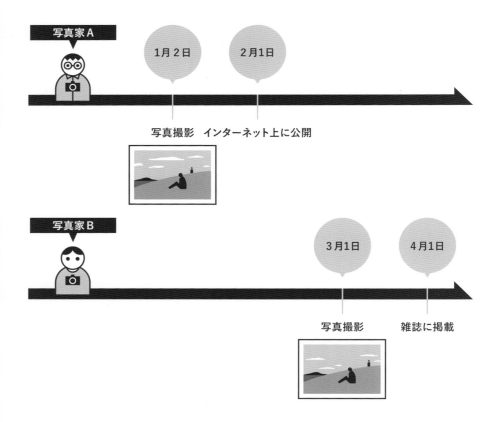

Case study

Q2-3. Considering how similar these two pieces of work are, was there any IP rights infringement in this situation? If so, who is the offender and which rights were violated?

Photographer A took a picture on January 2nd, then published it on the internet on February 1st. Photographer B took a very similar picture (see below the figures) on March 1st, then published it in a magazine on April 1st.

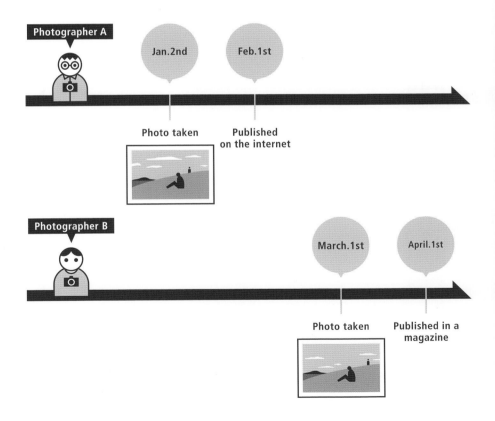

事例問題

Q3-1. これらは知的財産権侵害でしょうか？
侵害の場合、誰が何の権利を侵しているでしょうか？

企業Aは1月10日におもちゃの意匠を登録し、3月1日からその商品の販売を開始しました。企業Bは、2月1日に企業Aが登録した意匠に類似する商品（下図参照）の販売を開始しました。

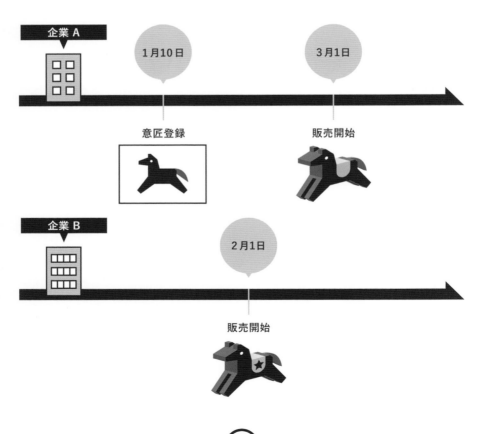

Case study

Q3-1. Considering how similar these two pieces of work are, was there any IP rights infringement in this situation? If so, who is the offender and which rights were violated?

On January 10th, Company A registered the design for their toy. The first unit of that product was sold on March 1st. Company B started selling a very similar toy (see below the figures) to Company A's Design right on February 1st.

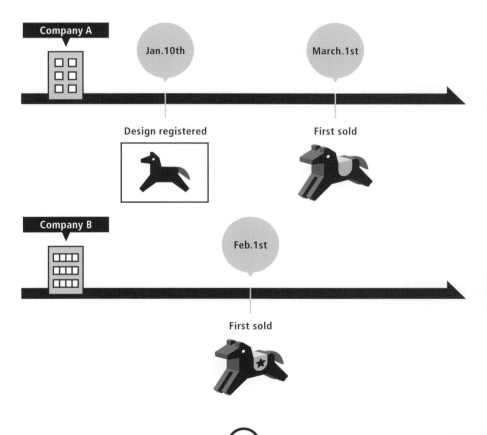

事例問題

Q3-2. これらは知的財産権侵害でしょうか?
侵害の場合、誰が何の権利を侵しているでしょうか?

企業Aは1月10日におもちゃの意匠を日本と米国で登録し、3月1日からその商品の販売を日本とフランスで開始しました。企業Bは、2月1日に企業Aが登録した意匠に類似する商品(下図参照)の販売を日本と中国で開始しました。また、4月1日には、ドイツで同じ商品の販売を開始しました。

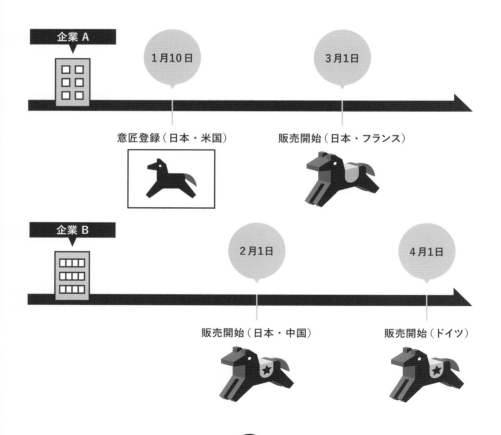

企業 A

1月10日

3月1日

意匠登録(日本・米国)

販売開始(日本・フランス)

企業 B

2月1日

4月1日

販売開始(日本・中国)

販売開始(ドイツ)

Case study

Q3-2. Considering how similar these two pieces of work are, was there any IP rights infringement in this situation? If so, who is the offender and which rights were violated?

On January 10th, Company A registered the design for their toy in Japan and in the USA. On March 1st, the first unit of that product was sold in Japan and France. Meanwhile, Company B started selling a very similar toy (see below the figures) in Japan and in China on February 1st, then on April 1st, they started selling it also in Germany.

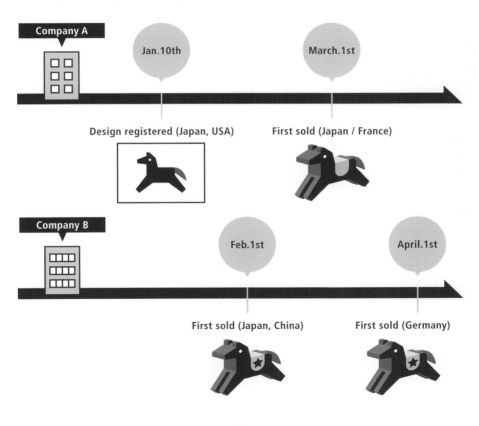

事例問題

Q3-3. これらは知的財産権侵害でしょうか？
侵害の場合、誰が何の権利を侵しているでしょうか？

企業Aは1月10日におもちゃの商品の販売を日本で開始しました。企業Bは、Aの商品を知った上で、2月1日に企業Aが販売した意匠に酷似する商品（下図参照）の販売を日本で開始しました。

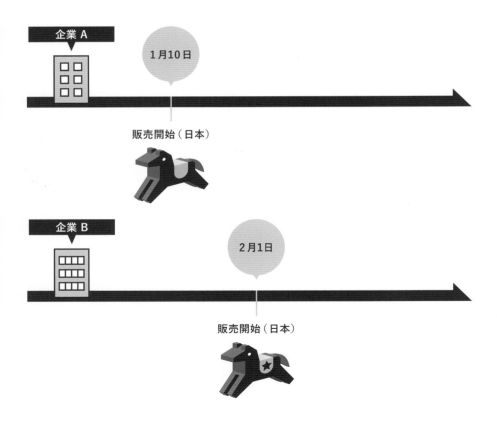

企業 A

1月10日

販売開始（日本）

企業 B

2月1日

販売開始（日本）

Case study

Q3-3. Considering how similar these two pieces of work are, was there any IP rights infringement in this situation? If so, who is the offender and which rights were violated?

On January 10th, Company A started selling their toy in Japan. On February 1st, Company B, which was familiar with A's product, started selling a very similar product (see below the figures) in Japan as well.

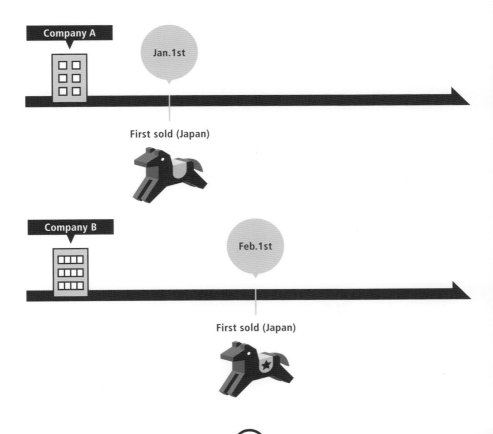

事例問題　回答

Case Study　Answers

著作物
（著作権の保護対象）

Q1. 日本の著作権法で保護されるものはどれでしょうか?

以下を記載してください。

保護されるもの：◯　保護されないもの：✕　どちらもあり得るもの：△

◯ 映画	△ 建築物	◯ 地図	✕ 書体
◯ 映画の脚本	◯ 写真	◯ 設計図面	△ ロゴマーク
◯ 音楽	◯ 小説	◯ 図表	✕ ブランド名
◯ 振り付け	◯ 論文	◯ 模型	◯ コンピューター プログラム
◯ パントマイム	◯ ゲーム	✕ 自動車	
◯ 絵画	◯ 漫画	✕ ボールペン	◯ データベース
◯ 彫刻		△ アイコン	

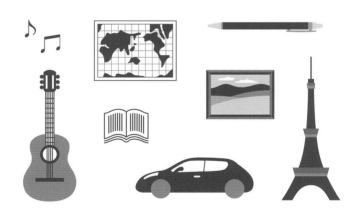

建築物は、東京タワー、都庁のビル、ベイブリッジのようなものは著作権法で保護されますが、量産化住宅は意匠法で保護され、著作権法では保護されません。

Objects Protected by Copyright Act

Q1. Which of these are protected under the Copyright Act in Japan?

Please mark according to the condition;

Protected : ○ Not protected : ✕ Both : △

○ Movies	△ Architecture	○ Maps	✕ Typefaces
○ Movie scripts	○ Photographs	○ Design drawings	△ Logo marks
○ Music	○ Novels	○ Charts	✕ Brand names
○ Choreography	○ Treatise	○ Models	○ Computer programs
○ Pantomime	○ Games	✕ Cars	
○ Paintings	○ Cartoons	✕ Ballpoint pens	○ Databases
○ Sculpture		△ Icons	

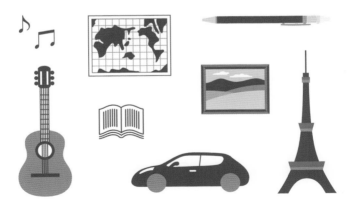

Unique structures such as Tokyo Tower, the Tokyo Metropolitan Government Building, and the Bay Bridge are protected by the Copyright Act. However, mass-produced houses or residences are protected by the Design Act and not the Copyright Act.

事例問題　回答

Q2-1. 侵害ではない

写真は著作物なので、著作権侵害に該当するか否かが問われている。写真家A,B 共に各自写真を撮影し、偶然酷似する作品を創作しているので、各自共に相手の著作権を侵害していない。

Q2-2. 侵害ではない

写真家BはAがインターネット上で写真を公開した後、酷似した写真を撮影している。この場合、BがAの写真を見て写真を撮影したとしても、写真を私的に使用する場合は問題ない。

Q2-3. 写真家BがAの著作権を侵害した可能性がある

写真家BはAがインターネット上で写真を公開した後、酷似した写真を撮影し、雑誌に掲載している。BがAの写真を見てそれに依拠して写真を撮影した場合は侵害が成立する。BがAの写真を知らずに偶然酷似した写真を撮影し、雑誌に掲載した場合は侵害とはならない。

Q3-1. 企業BはAの意匠権を侵害する

企業Aの意匠が登録された後、Bがその意匠権の意匠に類似する意匠の商品を販売したので、侵害となる。BがAの登録を知らなかった場合でも侵害となる。

Q3-2.

企業BはAの日本の意匠権を侵害する

Aが日本で意匠権を取得した後、Bはその意匠に類似する意匠の商品を日本での販売したため、BはAの日本の意匠権を侵害する。

企業Bはドイツでの販売について、AのEU統一意匠法の非登録意匠権を侵害する可能性がある。

AがEU域内であるフランスにおいて商品を販売した後、Bはその商品に類似する商品をEU域内であるドイツで販売した。EU統一意匠法はEU全域をカバーしている。

企業Aは中国において意匠権を取得していないため、Bの中国での販売は何ら権利を侵害していない。

Q3-3. 企業Bの販売行為は不正競争防止法違反である

企業Aが意匠権を取得していない場合でも、BがAの商品に依拠して酷似する商品を販売した場合、不正競争行為に該当する。

Case study Answers

Q2-1.No infringement

Photograph is protected by copyright, meaning that the question is whether photographer A or B made a Copyright infringement or not. A and B took the pictures by themselves and accidentally created very similar works, meaning in this case there was no infringement by either party.

Q2-2.No infringement

Photographer B shot a very similar photo to A's published photo on the internet. In this case, even if B sees A's photo and takes a similar picture, there is no problem if B uses that photo privately.

Q2-3.It is possible that Photographer B has infringed on A's copyright

Photographer B shot a very similar photo to A's and published it in a magazine after A had published that very similar photo on the internet. Infringement has occurred if B saw A's photo and B's photo is essentially based on A's work. If B accidentally took a very similar photo without seeing A's photo and publishes it in a magazine, then it will not be an infringement.

Q3-1.Company B infringes on the design right of A

After Company A's design has been registered, B sold a product of a similar design to A's design right and this becomes an infringement. Even if B is not aware of A's registration, it is still an infringement.

Q3-2.

Company B infringes on A's Japanese design right for sale in Japan.

After Company A's design has been registered in Japan, B sold a product of a similar design to A's design right in Japan and this becomes an infringement.

It is possible that Company B infringes on the UCD of A under the EU Design Act for sale in Germany.

First Company A sells the product in France (in EU) and after that B sells a similar product in Germany (in EU). Under the EU Design Act, even an unregistered design is protected across the EU.

Sales of Company B in China are not an infringement

Company A does not have a design right in China, so there is no problem in this specific case.

Q3-3.Company B's selling behavior is a violation of the Unfair Competition Prevention Act

Company B's selling behavior is a violation of the Unfair Competition Prevention Act.

Even if Company A does not have a design right, if B sells a product that closely resembles / is based on A's design, then it is deemed as an unfair competition.

基本用語
（日本語／英語）

参考URL

Basic Terms
（Japanese / English）

Reference URLs

基本用語（日英）

日本語 / Japanese		英語 / English
漢字 / Kanji	ローマ字 / Romaji	
ちてきざいさん 知的財産	chiteki zaisan	Intellectual Property (IP)
ちてきざいさんけん 知的財産権権	chiteki zaisan ken	Intellectual Property (IP) rights
ちょさくけん 著作権	chosaku ken	Copyright
とっきょけん 特許権	tokkyo ken	Patents
じつようしんあんけん 実用新案権	jitsuyo shin'an ken	Utility model rights
いしょうけん 意匠権	isho ken	Design rights
しょうひょうけん 商標権	shohyo ken	Trademarks
さんぎょうざいさんけん 産業財産権	sangyo zaisan ken	Industrial property rights
ちりてきひょうじ 地理的表示	chiriteki hyoji	Geographical indications (GI)
ふせいきょうそう 不正競争	fusei kyoso	Unfair competition
ちょさくけんほう 著作権法	chosakuken-ho	Copyright Act
とっきょほう 特許法	tokkyoho	Patent Act
じつようしんあんほう 実用新案法	jitsuyo shin'an-ho	Utility Model Act

Basic Terms (Japanese / English)

日本語 / Japanese		英語 / English
漢字 / Kanji	ローマ字 / Romaji	
いしょうほう 意匠法	ishoho	Design Act
しょうひょうほう 商標法	shohyoho	Trademark Act
ちりてきひょうじほう 地理的表示法	chiriteki hyojiho	Geographical Indications (GI) Act
ふせいきょうそうぼうしほう 不正競争防止法	fusei kyoso boshiho	Unfair Competition Prevention Act
にほんこくとっきょちょう 日本国特許庁	nihonkoku tokkyocho	Japanese Patent Office (JPO)
しゅつがん 出願	shutsugan	Filing / Application
とうろく 登録	toroku	Registration
しんさ 審査	shinsa	Examination
こうほう 公報	koho	Official gazette
せかいちてきしょゆうけんきかん 世界知的所有権機関	Sekai chiteki shoyuken kikan	World Intellectual Property Organization (WIPO)
ぱりじょうやく パリ条約	pari joyaku	Paris Convention
べるぬじょうやく ベルヌ条約	berunu joyaku	Bern Convention
けんりちょうさ 権利調査	kenri chosa	Search for the rights

参考 URL

日本 / Japan
日本国特許庁（特許権、実用新案権、意匠権、商標権） Japan Patent Office (JPO): patents, utility model rights, design rights, trademarks <div align="right">http://www.jpo.go.jp</div>
特許権、実用新案権、意匠権、商標権 調査データベース patents, utility model rights, design rights, trademarks search DB <div align="right">特許情報プラットフォーム - J-Plat Pat　https://www.j-platpat.inpit.go.jp</div>
文化庁 Agency for Cultural Affairs <div align="right">http://www.bunka.go.jp</div>
地理的表示に関する農林水産省HP Information about GI by MAFF (Ministry of Agriculture, Forestry and Fisheries) <div align="right">http://www.maff.go.jp/j/shokusan/gi_act/index.html</div>
地理的表示（GI）品の検索 Search for geographical indications (GI) products <div align="right">https://gi-act.maff.go.jp/</div>
不正競争防止法に関する経済産業省HP Information about Unfair Competition Prevetion Act By METI (Ministry of Economy, Trade and Industry) <div align="right">http://www.meti.go.jp/policy/economy/chizai/chiteki</div>

米国 / USA
米国特許商標庁 United States Patent and Trademark Office (USPTO) <div align="right">http://uspto.gov</div>
米国著作権庁 US Copyright Office <div align="right">https://www.copyright.gov</div>

Reference URLs

EU	
欧州連合（著作権） European Union (EU)	https://europa.eu
欧州特許庁（特許） European Patent Office (EPO): patents	https://www.epo.org/index.html
欧州知財庁（意匠権、商標権） European Union Intellectual Office (EUIPO): design rights, trademarks	https://euipo.europa.eu/
中国 / Caina	
国家版権局（著作権） National Copyright Administration of China (NCAC)	http://www.ncac.gov.cn
国家知識産権局（特許権（特許意匠権含む）、実用新案権、商標権） National Intellectual Property Administration, PRC (CNIPA): patents (including design patents), utility model rights, trademarks	http://english.cnipa.gov.cn/
https://www.wipo.int	WIPO の調査データベース / WIPO's Search DB
パテントスコープ（特許） PATENTSCOPE: Patents	https://patentscope2.wipo.int/search/ja/search.jsf
グローバルデザイン データベース（意匠権） Global Design Database: design rights	https://www.wipo.int/designdb/en
グローバルブランド データベース（商標権） Global Brand Database: trademarks	http://www.wipo.int/branddb/en

渡邉 知子 わたなべ ともこ

弁理士 / 横浜国立大学 客員教授

横浜国立大学において留学生および日本人を対象とした英語による知的財産権の講座「Plagiarism and its regulations」および「Business Planning and IP」を担当（2014年10月から現在）。他に専門家を含む社会人に対する講演（和英）なども行なっている。

日本大学芸術学部美術学科ビジュアルコミュニケーションデザイン専攻卒業。弁理士登録前は、通商産業技官として特許庁へ入庁後、意匠審査官として7年間審査に従事。

1997年7月弁理士登録後、2012年2月に渡邉知子国際特許事務所を設立し、継続的に知的財産権のコンサルティングを様々な企業に対し行なっている。

URL: www.watanabe-ipo.com

WATANABE Tomoko

Patent Attorney /
Guest Professor of Yokohama National University

Lectures for international and Japanese university students on IP rights in English, "Plagiarism and its regulations "and "Business Planning and IP" at Yokohama National University (October 2014 to present). Additionally instructs in Japanese and English for business professionals at other institutions.

Graduated from the Nihon University College of Art with a B.A. in Visual Communication Design. Joined the Japan Patent Office, part of the Ministry of International Trade and Industry, as a technical officer and worked as a design examiner for 7 years. Registered as a Patent Attorney in July,1997.

Established the WATANABE TOMOKO INTERNATIONAL PATENT OFFICE in February 2012. Provides IP consultation to a wide range of companies.

知的財産権のガイドブック
Intellectual Property Rights Guidebook

2020年5月1日　初版発行
Published First edition May 1st, 2020

著者 / Author	渡邊 知子 / WATANABE Tomoko
デザイン / Design	阿津 侑三 / AZU Yuzo
Special Thanks	小口 浩美 / OGUCHI Hiromi
	カリーナ・ノース / Karina North
	ロバート・リム / Robert Lim
	ルイーズ・ナガシマ / Louise Nagashima
	スチュアート・レニー / Stuart Rennie

発行・発行所 / Publication・Publisher　　一般社団法人 発明推進協会
Japan Institute for Promoting Invention and Innovation (JIPII)
105-0001 東京都港区虎ノ門 3-1-1
3-1-1, Toranomon, Minato-ku, Tokyo Japan 105-0001
Tel. + 81-3-3502-5433　編集 / Editing
　　 + 81-3-3502-5491　販売 / Sales
Fax.+ 81-3-5512-7567　販売 / Sales
URL. http://www.jiii.or.jp/

印刷 / Printed　　株式会社クレス / CRES Corporation